Praise for Jason Epstein's

EATING

"This convivial memoir by a distinguished publisher charts a lifetime of cooking and consumption. . . . Enlivening."　　　　　　　　　*—The New Yorker*

"What a storyteller! He brings food into the cultural experience in a beautiful way."　　　　*—Alice Waters*

"Epstein has such enthusiasm—yes, certainly for food but not only for what he has eaten and drunk—and he is adept at conveying this to the reader. . . . Will make many a reader's mouth water." *—The Washington Times*

"The conversational recipes and fond descriptions carry a clear intimation of how one should really live, the very thing that is so compelling in M. F. K. Fisher and Julia Child."　　 *—James Salter, coauthor of Life Is Meals*

"As Proust demonstrated with his madeleine, taste is a powerful unleasher of memories. Epstein's book, like M. F. K. Fisher's *The Art of Eating*, Laurie Colwin's *Home Cooking* and, more recently, Amanda Hesser's *Cooking for Mr. Latte*, tucks recipes into an entertaining, alternately informative and autobiographical narrative. . . . *Eating* . . . works for armchair cooks as well as active chefs, and has the advantage of being calorie-free."
　　　　　　　　　　　　　　 —San Francisco Chronicle

"It is delicious!"

—Maida Heatter, author of
Maida Heatter's Book of Great Desserts

"You'll want to gobble this slender volume in a single sitting. Go ahead—a little *Eating* is good for you."

—*The Free Lance-Star* (Fredericksburg, VA)

"Only a great editor could think up a new way to write a recipe. Jason Epstein's cookbook is really a short-story collection, in which the main character, Mr. Epstein, gets on with his life among writers and other hungry people of uncommon interest by cooking for them. It's all a seamless narrative, the tales of Epstein, in an apron at the gates of literature."

—Raymond Sokolov, author of
The Saucier's Apprentice

"*Eating* is a lovely read which I found made me hungry."

—Larry McMurtry, author of *Lonesome Dove*

"He writes with the voice and wisdom of a true cook. I love the connected way in which he understands the dialogue between ingredients, the process of cooking, and the conversation with the self. And of course I love the way in which he so clearly demonstrates that the practice of good cooking is really the practice of good living."

—Scott Peacock, coauthor of
The Gift of Southern Cooking

JASON EPSTEIN

EATING

Jason Epstein is the recipient of many awards, including the National Book Award for Distinguished Service to American Letters. For many years he was editorial director of Random House. He is the author of *Book Business: Publishing Past, Present, and Future.*

EATING

A MEMOIR

JASON EPSTEIN

ANCHOR BOOKS
A DIVISION OF RANDOM HOUSE, INC.
NEW YORK

FIRST ANCHOR BOOKS EDITION, OCTOBER 2010

Copyright © 2009 by Jason Epstein

All rights reserved. Published in the United States by Anchor Books, a division
of Random House, Inc., New York, and in Canada by Random House of
Canada Limited, Toronto. Originally published in hardcover by Alfred A. Knopf,
a division of Random House, Inc., New York, in 2009.

Anchor Books and colophon are registered trademarks of Random House, Inc.

This book is based on material that originally appeared in *The New York Times*.

Grateful acknowledgment is made to John Wiley & Sons, Inc., for permission to
reprint an excerpt from *The Art of Eating, 50th Anniversary Edition* by M. F. K. Fisher
and John Reardon, copyright © 1937, 1941, 1942, 1943, 1948, 1949, 1954, 1990, 2004
by M. F. K. Fisher. Reprinted by permission of John Wiley & Sons, Inc.

The Library of Congress cataloged the Knopf edition as follows:
Epstein, Jason.
Eating : a memoir / by Jason Epstein.—1st ed.
p. cm.
Includes index.
1. Cookery. 2. Gastronomy. 3. Epstein, Jason. I. Title.
TX652.E5923 2009
641.01'3—dc22   2009021217

Anchor ISBN: 978-1-4000-7825-7

Book design by Iris Weinstein

www.anchorbooks.com

Printed in the United States
10 9 8 7 6 5 4 3 2 1

Gratitude to the Unknown Instructors

What they undertook to do
They brought to pass;
All things hang like a drop of dew
Upon a blade of grass.

—W. B. YEATS

CONTENTS

PREFACE

I greatly admire Michael Pollan for his brave campaign to detoxify the American diet, but I lack the puritan fiber to be a true disciple. Of course I worry about the personal and environmental hazards that he and others have identified, and I mean to avoid them. Often I do, but not always, for though my will is strong my temptations are stronger, as they were on a lovely late-summer day recently on eastern Long Island at the height of the blueberry season.

With Michael Pollan in mind, I promised myself that this year I would not make a blueberry pie with its simple sugars, animal fats, and refined flour, as I had been doing for years at blueberry time, which coincides with my birthday. This year, as always, my children and grandchildren were coming from far away to celebrate the occasion, and that morning I stopped at the Pike Farm Stand to pick up some vegetables for dinner: tomatoes, sweet corn, cauliflower, and so on. I included two and a half quarts of blueberries, just the amount for a pie, but vowed not to pour them into a bowl, as I had done on so many previous birthdays, and mix in a cup or a little more of sugar, some lemon juice, or, better yet, the zest, and enough powdered cinnamon so that its faint aroma rises as the pie bakes, and then shower the mixture with arrowroot to hold the juice without making the berries gummy, as cornstarch does. On previous birthdays I would roll out on a marble slab two very thin sheets of the simplest pastry, the one for the bottom slightly smaller than the one for the top. To make the pastry, I cut a quarter-pound of unsalted butter in the food processor into two and a half cups of all-purpose flour with a little sugar and less salt, until the butter was incorporated but still a little lumpy. Then very carefully I added a half-cup of cold water a little at a time until the dough began to form. Though most cookbooks suggest letting the dough rest awhile to relax the gluten, I have never found this step necessary. I fitted one sheet of pastry into a black ten-inch pie tin with holes in the bottom, poured the filling onto it, and topped the berries with the other sheet, into which I poked a few slits, then sealed the edge and brushed the top with egg wash. After forty-five minutes or so in a 375-degree oven, the egg-glazed pie with its rivulets of blueberry syrup would be ready. But this year I vowed to serve the blueberries plain, or perhaps with a little crème Chantilly and a plate of cookies.

Instead I made a pie. I served it still warm beneath vanilla ice cream hand-cranked by my friend Billy Leonard in his old White Mountain freezer. This followed a dinner of ripe local tomatoes and fried chicken from Sal Iacono's farm, with a bowl of steamed cauliflower picked that morning. I let the glorious cauliflower speak for itself, with neither salt nor butter.

On the other hand, I would not dream of making the French toast that my daughter, Helen, recalled when I asked recently about her childhood culinary memories. This monstrous concoction I learned to make when I worked many years ago in the kitchen of a boys' camp in Maine, from a cook named George who worked winters in a logging camp. He showed me how to dip a thick slice of homemade *pain de mie* in pancake batter with a little extra baking powder, fry it in deep fat till it puffs, browns nicely, and forms a lacy fringe of fried batter, dip it in a mixture of sugar and cinnamon, and cover it with maple syrup. I mention this deadly pleasure here as temptation's outer boundary. No one who reads this book should think of going near it.

I began cooking as a child as other children of my generation toyed with chemistry sets or electric trains. I remember reading Irma Rombauer when I was ten or so with the same curiosity that I read Kipling and Jules Verne. My mother had little interest in cooking, and my father none at all, so I was free to amuse myself in the kitchen without getting in their way. Later, I worked a bit in restaurants, where I picked up fragments of technique and jargon and began to think of myself as a cook long before anyone else might have agreed. As readers of this book will see, I prefer plain cooking. I don't bother with foams, complex emulsions, or exotic ingredients, but let each ingredient speak for itself, often with the help of herbs, spices, and wine. I am a serviceable cook. Friends like what I serve them and come back for more. This gives me pleasure.

Recipes are approximations, starting points. I learn

usually by failing the first time, then discovering where I went wrong, then trying again, and so on, until the basic preparation becomes second nature. Then I vary it, as I plan to do tonight with swordfish in a spicy marinara, an easy dish to make for ten or twelve people. I make the marinara early in the day, and sear the fish quickly at dinnertime in olive oil, and top it with the sauce just before it goes to the table (page 83). For the marinara tonight—actually a kind of puttanesca—I'm thinking of mashing in some fresh sardines if I can find them, a Sicilian touch, along with the pine nuts and raisins that are already in the sauce. I won't risk the whole pot of marinara, but try a cupful with only a bit of sardine. It may not work—the sardine may be too strong, may squelch the lively marinara—but it's worth a try. When I made this the first time, I let the sautéed swordfish sit for a while in the marinara, with the result that the sauce, which had been fairly tight, became watery and the swordfish dry.

The value of writers like Michael Pollan, whom every cook should read, is that they suggest limits which we may respect or ignore as we choose—but at the extreme they define the reality by whose rules we succeed or fail, live or die. I look forward to next year's blueberry season, and now that apple season is here I may bake a tarte tatin (page 163) now and then; otherwise, except for special occasions, I'll skip dessert.

In this book, when I recommend olive oil I mean extra-virgin unless otherwise indicated. There are many types of extra-virgin oil, and many shops let you taste before you buy. Take advantage of this opportunity. Fine-quality oils come in many flavors and textures, from subtle to aromatic, from gentle to powerful. As with wine, let your taste be your guide.

My thanks to:

An incomplete list of my instructors, in no particular order, includes Michael Field, Elizabeth David, Julia Child, Alice Waters, Daniel Boulud, Irma Rombauer, Maida Heatter, Frankie Pellegrino, Patrick O'Connell, Fernand Point, Rick Moonen, Julia Reed, Mario Batali, Wolfgang Puck (whose original Spago, with its bare pine walls and Milton Berle always in the corner, is dear to my memory), Joël Robuchon, Mike Anthony, Buwei Chao, Lou, Marie, and Sal "Di Palo," Mark Russ Federman, Alice Toklas, Richard Olney, Paula Wolfert, Diana Kennedy, Martin and Adela Garcia, Sheila Lukins, Pierre Franey, Charlie Palmer, Eddie Schoenfeld, and that centuries-long procession of unknown cooks and bakers from whom my teachers and their teachers learned their craft.

I thank Billy Norwich for suggesting that I write a recipe column for the Style section of *The New York Times,* from which much of this book derives. I thank, too, my dear and second-oldest friend on earth, the incomparable Judith Jones, for urging me to use these recipes as the basis for a book. Thanks to Terry Zaroff-Evans for her superb copyediting, and to Carol Carson for the splendid jacket. Also my agent, Andrew Wylie, for reminding me that this book was long overdue; my wife, Judy Miller, for reading and commenting on the manuscript; and Jacob Epstein, Susie Norris, Helen Epstein, Barbara Goldsmith, Mary Bahr, Hilton Als, Doron Weber, and Olaf Olafsson, who also found the time in their very busy lives to read and comment.

SAG HARBOR, NEW YORK, SEPTEMBER 13, 2008

EATING

A MEMOIR

ONE

COOKING
AS
STORYTELLING

I seldom cook by numbers, any more than when I walk my dog, Hamlet, along the familiar streets of lower Manhattan I use a compass or plot my course on a map. When my wife, Judy, or friends ask how much of this or that I use in a stew or salad, I say "a little" or "a lot," but usually I say "not too much"—not meaning to be rude, but because I agree with the ancient Greek philosopher Heraclitus that you cannot enter the same river twice, that each act is unique and irretrievable, like the water rushing downriver to the sea, or the seconds of our lives ticking away on our wrists, or the way we hear a tune or read a book. From a Heraclitean perspective, it is impossible to make the same dish twice—nor should one want to, since it can be made better the next time, when you will be a little wiser and the ingredients, a little more forthcoming. Recipes should be more like stories than like maps or formulae. So in this book I tell practical stories about some favorite dishes and how they fit into my life and hope readers will try them in the same spirit. In cooking, "not too much" is usually a good rule, since you seldom want a particular flavor to dominate. You want harmony, though syncopation helps.

I am a book publisher, not a professional cook, though in my youth I worked in restaurant kitchens, and later published many fine books by famous chefs who became friends—Alice Waters, Wolfgang Puck, Daniel Boulud, Maida Heatter, and Patrick O'Connell, among others—and learned from them, too. From time to time I've written about food for various publications, and many of the dishes I describe in this book appeared first in those magazines, usually with a list of ingredients and step-by-step instructions for combining them. But in this book I shall describe some favorite dishes as if I were talking to friends who have liked something I've cooked and want to try it themselves. To friends I would not dream of reciting a list of measured ingredients and numbered instructions. Except when it comes to baking, where precision is important, I prefer to suggest parameters and leave it to others to work out for themselves such specifics as time, quantity, and temperatures, so that the dish becomes theirs, too. Cooking is like poetry, where one's unique voice is everything: words and their placement are essential ingredients, too, but the poet's own voice makes them sing, which is why when you paraphrase a poem you end up with nothing but words.

For example, take a simple penne in tomato sauce

with basil and mozzarella, which I often make for friends at lunch.

PENNE IN TOMATO SAUCE For three or four people you will need a twenty-eight-ounce can of San Marzano tomatoes. These are grown in volcanic soil on the slopes of Vesuvius and sold in high-quality supermarkets and Italian fine-food shops. I buy mine at Di Palo's magnificent cheese shop on Grand Street in lower Manhattan, a few blocks from where I live. From a culinary point of view, Di Palo's is as close to a visit to Italy as you will get without leaving home. San Marzanos are more plump than other varieties, with more tomato flavor and just enough acidity. But if you can't find San Marzanos, any good brand will do, preferably Italian. Muir Glen is a good American brand.

For the sauce, heat just enough extra-virgin olive oil to cover the bottom of a heavy pot large enough to hold a pound of cooked penne. As the oil warms but before it begins to shimmer, add two or three cloves of slivered garlic, and a minute later a medium-size jalapeño, minced, its seeds removed. Then reduce the flame to its lowest point. The idea is to infuse the oil with the various flavors over a very low flame until the fragrance fills the kitchen but before the jalapeño begins to brown. If it does brown a little, don't worry. But keep an opened can of tomatoes nearby, to add as soon as the garlic mixture softens and the aroma rises from the pan. If you turn your back for a minute and the jalapeño blackens or the garlic becomes acrid, toss it out and start over. After you've chopped the jalapeño, wash your hands lest you inadvertently rub your eye.

If your tomatoes are watery and shapeless, throw them out and try another brand. To the tomatoes, add one or two tablespoons of dried oregano and reduce over a medium flame. Fresh oregano, if you have some in your garden, will give the dish a perfumed lift, but it is much less intense than the dried. You will have to strip from its stems more than twice as much as the dry for the fragrance to take hold: a chore perhaps not worth the effort. The sauce will thicken as the water evaporates in ten or fifteen minutes. It should be somewhat tight. If it thickens too much, add a little water. If it is too watery, reduce it further or it will not grip the pasta. Then add coarse sea salt and pepper to taste, adding the salt carefully, a few grains at a time, until the sauce comes smartly and suddenly to life. Some cooks add a little sugar or soften carrot and onion with the garlic and pepper. I usually don't. The San Marzano tomatoes are sweet enough.

HERBS   It is much less expensive and more convenient to buy dried herbs such as oregano, basil, sage, and so on, by the pound, rather than in little bottles—or, depending on how much you are likely to use, a half year's supply. Most dried herbs remain fragrant for several months, either in the sealed containers in which they are sold or in your own airtight canisters. Throw stale herbs out at once. They will ruin your sauce. I order from kalustyan.com, whose wonderful shop is on Lexington Avenue in New York, or sausagemaker.com in Buffalo, New York.

Meanwhile, fill a large pot halfway with water, and add salt until you can just begin to taste it. Then bring the salted water to a rapid boil and add a pound of dried or fresh penne, either ridged (rigate) or smooth, preferably an Italian brand. I keep a small bowl of cool water nearby so that as the penne cooks I can extract a few pieces with a slotted spoon or tongs, drop them in the cool water, and taste them without burning my mouth. Fresh pasta will take only a few minutes to cook, so watch it carefully lest it turn to mush. Dried pasta may take as many as seven or eight minutes, though some imported dried pastas cook almost as quickly as fresh, so, unless you've used the brand before, taste and be careful not to overcook it. It should be firm to the bite—al dente—before you add it to the tomato sauce, where it will cook a little more. When the pasta is ready, lift it out with a long-handled strainer—the Chinese version is best. Toss the strained penne into the thickened, warm sauce, and with a wooden spoon mix it about until the pasta is well coated. The idea is to flavor the penne, rather than think of the sauce as the main ingredient and the pasta as its conveyance. Discard the pasta water if you plan to serve the penne at once. If you choose to serve the pasta later, save the water, bring it to a boil, and ladle some slowly into the pasta as you reheat it over a moderate flame until the penne loosens. The pasta will no longer be al dente, but will be edible nonetheless. Serve very hot in large pasta bowls. Top each bowl generously with hand-shredded—not chopped—fresh basil, and cube for each serving a small handful of the freshest possible mozzarella, being careful that the cheese rests upon the basil leaves and not the hot pasta, lest the cheese melt and become stringy. Use only very fresh mozzarella, made the same day. Avoid the plastic-wrapped product sold in supermarket coolers. You may prefer buffalo mozzarella from Italy for a tangier flavor. Unlike mozzarella made from cow's milk, which toughens as it ages, buffalo mozzarella becomes sharp and softens with age. Dieters should know that it takes four quarts of whole milk to make a pound of mozzarella. In this recipe, a half-pound cubed should be enough for four.

The secret is the jalapeño, which adds subtle heat from the bottom up and intensifies the other flavors. You will not notice it at once, but it will be awaiting you at the back of your tongue. If instead of jalapeño you use dried Italian red pepper flakes, the heat will be less subtle, though a quick dusting of a few flakes reduced to a powder by your fingertips before you add the basil and mozzarella complements the jalapeño from the top down. Another secret is the cool mozzarella contrasting with the hot, peppery pasta and spicy basil. I have seldom served this to anyone—even dieters—who didn't ask for more until there was none left.

SPAGHETTINI OR LINGUINE WITH CLAMS

Spaghettini or linguine with clams is another simple dish, too often made to seem complicated. All you need is a pound of pasta; two or three garlic cloves, peeled; a jalapeño, finely chopped; just enough olive oil in which to heat the garlic and pepper; two cups of dry white wine; some Italian parsley; and, for two people, two dozen littleneck (small, hard-shell) clams, rinsed, or, much preferably, two pounds of manilla clams if you can find them (and if you can't, look for New Zealand cockles, a close relative). Manillas are sweeter than little-necks and used widely in Italy. Dried red pepper flakes are optional. Fill a stockpot half full of water, add salt, and bring to a boil. Meanwhile, heat a little olive oil in a heavy-bottomed pot just large enough to accommodate a pound of cooked pasta and the clams, and add the whole garlic and chopped jalapeño and cook gently until the garlic and pepper soften. Add the wine, and reduce quickly by half. Then add the clams, cover the pot, and when the clams open, after a few minutes, remove the cover and turn off the flame. Add the pasta to the boiling stockpot, and when it is al dente (see page 7), lift it with tongs and add it to the clam sauce. Coat the linguine or spaghettini with the sauce, and put in large pasta bowls. Sprinkle with coarsely chopped Italian parsley and serve. A sprinkling of red pepper flakes and a dash of extra-virgin olive oil are optional. If the pasta seems dry, add a ladle or two of hot pasta water. This quantity will serve two, maybe three.

Since we're on the subject of pasta, I should mention the irresistible Bolognese ragù from the great Mario Ba-tali's *Babbo Cookbook*, which I have somewhat modified.

BOLOGNESE SAUCE This is one of the all-time great ragùs, and easy to make after a little trial and error. Again, you will need a pot large enough for the rather substantial sauce and a pound of imported tagliatelle, Spinosi brand if you can find it. Batali uses pappardelle, and you may, too. In the pot, heat a little olive oil and soften a few chopped garlic cloves with some diced onion, carrot, and celery. Then cube a quarter-pound of pancetta (unsmoked Italian bacon) or, preferably, guanciale, cured from hog cheeks but not smoked, if you can find it in your Italian specialty store, and spin the cubes for a few seconds in a food processor. Scrape the pancetta or guanciale into the pot, and stir until it begins to melt. Then crumble a pound each of ground veal and pork into the pot and over a medium-hot flame brown the meats. Then toss in a small handful of dried oregano leaves, and mix everything together. Batali calls for a small can of tomato paste at this point, or use three generous tablespoons of strattu instead.

STRATTU If you can find in your Italian market an infinitely more fragrant tomato concentrate called strattu (that is, extract) get it. It's expensive and not easy to find—Di Palo stocks it—but strattu will send your ragù directly to the empyrean.

Now add a cup of milk and another of white wine, reduce the flame to a simmer, cover the pot loosely, and let it simmer over the lowest flame for an hour or so, checking from time to time that the sauce hasn't dried out and begun to burn. Add more milk and wine as necessary. Add sea salt and fresh-ground pepper to taste carefully. Then sprinkle a good handful of very fragrant fresh thyme leaves, from the garden if you have one, into the ragù. Meanwhile, bring a large pot of salted water to a boil, cook a pound of tagliatelle until it's al dente, and transfer the pasta with tongs to the ragù and mix thoroughly, saving the pasta water if you're not planning to serve the ragù immediately (see page 7). Drop a tong-full into each large pasta bowl, sprinkle with grated parmigiana, and serve while hot. The dish is even better the second day, as leftovers.

In childhood, I became interested in cooking as I watched my grandmother Ida bake pies, preserve peaches and applesauce from her own trees, and roast chickens that she had fattened herself in the cellar when it was too cold for them outdoors. My grandparents' old house, atop a steep hill in Auburn, Maine, had a primitive coal-burning furnace which kept the cellar warm but didn't do much on icy days for the big, drafty parlors, despite heavy wood-framed storm windows. Ida was tall, handsome, and amiable. She carried herself with dignity and smiled often and easily. She was not a great cook and not always even a very good one, but she tried. Her grandchildren respected and loved her and went along with the pretense that her food was delicious. Or perhaps, being children, they didn't know any better. At the age of ten, I did know better, for my parents would often take me with them when they dined out with friends on Sundays at country inns—including the Toll House, with its famous cookies—around Boston, where we lived when we were not visiting my grandparents in Maine.

My grandmother was from Russia and said she liked cold houses with warm kitchens. Her husband, my grandfather, was born prematurely and kept in a shoe box wrapped in fur until he was old enough to survive, or so I was told. When I knew him in old age, he wore in winter what was called a pelt, a stiff canvas coat lined with a sheepskin, an echo, I thought, of his primitive incubator. On bitter winter days when the frost formed peaks on the storm windows in the unheated parlor, my cousins and I sat in the kitchen warmed by the big woodstove with its nickel trim and the words "Model: Home Fireside" in raised letters above a temperature gauge on the oven door.

Prospect Hill, where my grandparents lived, was almost perpendicular, and with my friend Raymond Begin, who was smart and funny and spoke French—he would become a Roman Catholic priest in Canada—I skied down it on heavy wooden Norwegian skis with knobs at the tip. Then, with sealskins attached to our skis, we would herringbone back up. Afterward we would go across South Main Street to Cloutier's store (pronounced "Cloochies") for frozen Milky Ways and root beer.

On stormy winter mornings, you could see from my grandmother's kitchen windows the windswept snow swirl against the blackness of Mr. Jackson's open barn doors across the road. Pete, my grandparents' old English bulldog, slept on a braided rug in front of the stove, so that my grandmother had to pirouette awkwardly around him as she lifted her roasts and pies from the oven. From my perch next to the stove, atop the big box painted blue with a slanted top, like a saltbox, where the firewood was kept, I effortlessly absorbed from my beaming grandmother, with her Oxford glasses on their gold chain, the ambience of warmth and safety from which the desires of a lifetime were formed, including the desire that persists long after her death to help her improve her cooking. Like the walls and ceiling of my New York kitchen today, hers were wainscoted, but the varnish was older and mellower than mine. The copper plumbing must have been added after the house was built, since it was bracketed to the walls rather than embedded in them, and it rattled and groaned whenever the brass faucets were opened over the heavy slate sink.

In summertime, when the kitchen became uncomfortably warm and the fumes of melting tar rising from the street clutched at our throats, I would retreat with a book to a cool pantry just off the kitchen which my grandmother called her "shed," its walls lined with her preserves in gleaming jars: crab apples, peaches, cucumbers, pie fillings, hot peppers, eggplant, green tomatoes. Since I don't recall ever being served any of these preserves, I assume the handsome jars were meant for display. My grandmother had an eye for décor. The floor was covered with old patchwork quilts where Pete slept in the summer, and where, under a single dim bulb hanging from a wire, I read the novels of R. L. Stevenson and E. Nesbit, and, with difficulty, *The Pickwick Papers* and *A Tale of Two Cities* in an edition given to subscribers to the local newspaper. I still associate these novels of Dickens with my grandmother's shed and Pete the bulldog growling softly in his dreams beside me.

My grandmother was born to a prosperous family of Odessa grain merchants who later fell on hard times. She was not meant to be a cook, or a gardener, either. Instead of arranging her plants in rows, she grew them wherever it suited her and them: rhubarb beside the barn, dill by the front door, cabbages beside the hydrangea, rutabaga in the orchard. Her family in the Crimea had been able to keep servants, educate their children, and move in style, first to Argentina and then to the United States, where her father, a grim, bearded presence in an oval frame in the front parlor, speculated in ostrich feathers and lost everything in the Panic of '07. His wife hung beside him in the parlor, scowling, almond-eyed, and padded like an old samurai.

My grandmother was a brave and cheerful soul and did her best to maintain a certain tone, particularly at mealtime. But some of her special dishes I recall to this day with dismay, especially her chicken pot pie made from a worn-out laying hen. The crust, shiny on top, was gummy underneath, the broth was thin, and the chicken itself overcooked, dry, stringy, and tasteless. Yet our family romance declared her chicken pie a favorite, and my cousins and I dutifully cheered when my dear, beaming grandmother brought the pie in from the kitchen. She had an infectious gift for conviviality. So when the family gathered around her big, round golden-oak dining-room table there was joy despite the pie. She wanted us to be happy, and we were eager to accommodate her belief that the pie made us so.

Over the years, with the help of *Fannie Farmer* and *The Settlement Cook Book,* her repertory improved. I remember in summertime bowls of coleslaw, beet soup, platters of fried or roasted chicken, peach, apple, and blueberry pies; in winter, double brisket and braised parsnips, breast of veal stuffed with Swiss chard, lamb shank and shoulder braised slowly for hours, caramelized, falling off the bone, and ginger cookies. My grandparents were ethnically Jewish but unobservant freethinkers who spoke a Yankee-inflected Yiddish with a few French Canadian exclamations among themselves, and a Yiddish-inflected Yankee to us. "I reckon," my grandfather, who wore fireman's suspenders and canvas trousers, would say when he meant "yes." On Jewish holidays, my grandmother cooked for the synagogue, having convinced her neighbors, as she had convinced herself, that she was a superior cook. On those occasions, her chickens had to be killed and dressed according to Jewish ritual. It was my job to stuff three or four of her plump fowl into burlap bags and carry them live down Prospect Hill to the ritual butcher, who, in dim light under a low ceiling in a windowless cellar, slit their throats, left them to bleed into a funnel, and handed them over to be plucked by a hunched figure all but invisible in a dark corner, as in a Rembrandt etching. Some years later, I helped my older cousin Leon, who was enrolled in Columbia College, where I would later study, carry a set of Macaulay's *History of England,* which he had found in a secondhand bookshop, up the hill.

The books were heavier than the chickens. Climbing up Prospect Hill with chickens and books—a prelude to my life.

Today, with fair-quality farm-raised chicken breasts, skinned and boned, in the supermarket, and inexpensive chicken parts to enrich the organic broth sold in cartons, there is no excuse for a dry and tasteless chicken pot pie.

CHICKEN POT PIE First I bake separately a puff-pastry disk a little bigger than the circumference of the cocotte in which I make the filling. I bake the pastry between two sheet pans to form a crunchy, buttery, waferlike crust barely a quarter-inch thick.

I begin with two and a half cups of all-purpose flour, a pinch of salt, and half a stick of cold, unsalted butter, roughly chopped in chunks, all whirled together in a food processor until the butter is incorporated into the flour but still a little lumpy.

Then I add a scant half-cup or so of cold water a little at a time and pulse off and on quickly until the dough begins to form a firm, crumbly paste, which I scoop from the processor, form into a ball, and flatten into a rectangle. You may want to wrap the dough in foil and let it rest for twenty minutes in the refrigerator, long enough for the gluten to relax, but I don't bother with this step. If the dough is too crumbly, I add a little water and knead it into the dough. If it's too wet, I knead in a little flour. Next I roll this dough out on a cool marble slab into an oblong about an eighth of an inch thick, and cut and shape a quarter-pound of unsalted butter into a somewhat smaller and thinner oblong, which I center atop the pastry. Then I fold the dough in thirds—like a letter—around the butter, crimping the edges so that the butter is completely enclosed.

Now I turn the dough with its butter filling ninety degrees, roll it out again as an oblong, and fold and repeat the process for six turns, being careful at each turn to keep the butter tightly sealed. You can keep track of the turns by marking each with a thumbprint. You must work quickly, in a cool kitchen, or the butter will melt. To avoid this, chill the dough in the refrigerator after each turn. This will keep the butter firm and give the gluten a chance to relax, so that the dough won't spring back when you roll it out. I use an old-fashioned glass rolling pin, actually a bottle that can be filled with ice water, with a glass handle at either end. Finally, with a very sharp knife (or a pizza wheel), I cut the dough into a round whose circumference is slightly larger than that of the pot in which I will make the pie filling, being sure to crimp the edges to keep the butter from leaking out. With the oven at

PUFF PASTRY Many supermarkets carry ready-made frozen puff pastry, and it's important, unless you decide to make your own, to find a brand made with butter rather than vegetable shortening. I like to make my own puff pastry, but when I'm in a hurry I look for the Dufour brand in the supermarket freezer. Be careful, however: it doesn't always keep well in your home freezer. Making your own, on the other hand, is not as difficult as you may think.

425 degrees, I then cut a circle of parchment paper the size of the pastry circle and lay it on a baking sheet and lay the pastry atop the paper, pricking a few holes in it here and there. Then I lay another round of parchment paper atop the pastry, place a second baking sheet atop the second parchment, and bake the pastry for about fifteen minutes, until crisp and beginning to brown. Next I reduce the heat to 350 degrees and bake for another fifteen minutes, being careful not to let the crust burn. I roll out and bake the scraps in ornamental shapes. This is less complicated than it sounds; nevertheless, you may prefer Dufour or another brand made with butter, in which case follow the instructions in the package.

For the filling, you will need two approximately sixteen-ounce skinless and boneless organic chicken breasts, cut into one-inch cubes. Pat the cubes dry with a paper towel and toss them in two tablespoons of heated but not smoking vegetable oil in a heavy Dutch oven or cocotte until light brown but not cooked through, and set aside. Clean the pot, melt two tablespoons of butter in the clean pot, and add a dozen or so pearl onions. (You can peel them easily by trimming the stem end and placing them in a lightly oiled pan in a 400-degree oven for ten minutes until soft and lightly browned. When they are cool, slip off the skins.) Set the onions aside with the chicken cubes and add to the pot a cup of diced carrots, a cup of diced celery, a sweet onion neatly diced, and a half-pound of bite-size cremini or other interesting mushrooms. Small chanterelles or morels, if you can find them, are ideal. Or use small white mushrooms.

Add butter as needed. Sauté carrots and celery with the onions and mushrooms until soft and slightly colored, and set aside with the pearl onions and chicken.

Meanwhile, in a separate pot, bring four cups of strong, defatted homemade chicken broth to a boil, or reduce six cups of organic stock from a carton, enriched with chicken parts and defatted, to four cups. Clean the cocotte once more, and in it melt six tablespoons of butter. Whisk in three tablespoons or so of Wondra instant-blending flour or arrowroot, and cook, stirring, until just turning light brown, then whisk in the boiling stock, smoothing out the lumps, and one and a half cups of half and half, three or four tablespoons to taste of dry sherry, chopped leaves from a stem of fresh rosemary, and a tablespoon each of fragrant fresh thyme and Italian parsley. Add sea salt and fresh-ground pepper to taste and the juice of two lemons. Bring to a slow boil, reduce, and simmer until the sauce is thick enough to coat a spoon. If it's too thick, thin it with more stock and/or half and half. Cover the pot with parchment or plastic wrap until ready to serve. If using fresh peas, cook them first over a low flame in a small pot with a few lettuce leaves and a little butter, but do not add water. When they begin to soften, remove and discard the lettuce leaves and add the peas to the reserved chicken and vegetables. Otherwise, defrost and add a box of frozen peas. When ready to serve, remove the parchment or plastic wrap. Stir in the chicken and vegetables, and heat gently over moderate heat, being careful not to overcook the chicken or burn the sauce. When the chicken is just cooked through and firm to the touch, taste the sauce, correct the sherry, lemon juice, salt, and pepper, and turn off the flame. Return the pastry to a moderate oven until warm. Then cut it with a sharp knife into as many wedges as there are guests. Use the scraps for seconds. Serve the pie, which will serve six for dinner or eight for lunch, sprinkled with flat parsley, coarsely chopped, in large, warm pasta bowls, with the puff-pastry wedge pointed down into the sauce. I myself plate the pie with the puff-pastry wedges already in place, but others might bring the whole pie to table with the wedges on a separate platter.

When I was asked by a magazine editor some years ago to describe my kitchen, it struck me for the first time that I had unconsciously re-created my grandmother's wainscoted and varnished walls and ceilings, big black stove, cherrywood countertops, yellow pine floors, willowware platters, and bright copper pots. This cannot have been accidental, for I have two kitchens—one in Manhattan, where I have a shelf for preserves, and the other in Sag Harbor on Long Island, and each is a collage of the other. In the Sag Harbor kitchen, my favorite perch is a blue armchair. My chicken pot pie is homage to my indomitable grandmother.

I have never taken much stock in psychoanalysis, with its contribution to narcissism and its emphasis on repressed memory. I believe that the important roots of human suffering are to be found within the shared failings of the species itself—in the human condition—

modified by personal genetic determinants, rather than in the accidental encounters of one's childhood. Yet my preference for varnished wainscoting, for the robin's-egg-blue kitchen armchair where I like to read, and my choice of the kitchen as a place in which not only to cook and eat but also to read, write, and contemplate the world, as well as my reflexive association to this day of England's great Whig historian with a plucked chicken wrapped in a Yiddish newspaper, suggest that I have been too quick to dismiss Dr. Freud's talking cure. My lifelong interest in re-creating the cuisine of my childhood is proof of the persistence of memory and its power to shape one's days.

TWO

THE PERSISTENCE
OF MEMORY

When William Wordsworth wrote "The Child is father of the Man," he knew what he was talking about. The warmth of my grandmother's stove on snowbound days, and the summer days when I read Dickens in her shed with its gleaming jars of pickled beets and applesauce determined the life to come. To these shaping memories was added a few years later a simple hamburger, barely a half-inch thick, charred at the edges, on a toasted bun, and eaten with a slice of sweet onion by a lakeside shack in Winthrop, Maine, at dusk, amid the August hum of crickets. Macnamara's stand, with its fragrant raw-pine walls and neat hand-lettered sign on a canoe paddle above the immaculate screen door painted white, is long gone, replaced by an access ramp to the new Augusta highway. But the memory of those magical hamburger evenings beside the lake is fixed in my mind as firmly as my own name.

Macnamara's shack occupied a well-lighted grass plot between Lake Maranacook and the old Augusta Road where I spent some boyhood summers during the War. In August, we toiled from dawn until dusk in the hot fields, picking snap beans, which we stuffed into burlap sacks and tossed onto trucks for the cannery that shipped them overseas to the troops. On Fridays, when we were paid at the end of the day, still in our bib overalls and shoeless, we paddled our canoes into town and spent our wages on hamburgers, Nehi, and frozen Milky Ways. Our leftover nickels went into Macnamara's jukebox: Vera Lynn, Artie Shaw, Glenn Miller, the Andrews Sisters. We were fourteen that summer of 1942, our front teeth still too big for our sunburned faces. Under bare bulbs strung over Macnamara's outdoor counter, with its neat arrangements of ketchup and mustard bottles, salt and pepper shakers, and paper napkins, we were proud of our war work. Like victorious warriors after battle, we ate our hamburgers in the hazy twilight, and after dark raced our canoes home across the lake.

The memory of those evenings would outlast the century and provoke a futile quest to recapture the fugitive joys fixed in mind's wanderings by those hamburgers beside Lake Maranacook.

Later, there were other hamburgers, but none so memorable. In the 1950s and '60s, at the Hamburger Heaven chain in New York, the hamburger was a plump sirloin pillow, and the bun sturdy enough not to disintegrate in one's hands, as today's supermarket buns will do unless the burger is cooked through. In those genteel surroundings, where Holly Golightly might occupy the next seat, one was served at the counter or at seats along the wall with hinged trays, like infants' high-chair trays, by stately black waiters in white coats who delivered our hamburgers like a sacrament with ketchup and bowls of sweet pepper relish and raw onion. After lunch on days when the *Queens* or *Caronia* had landed, I would walk across Park Avenue to the Holliday Bookshop to buy the latest Henry Green or Ivy Compton-Burnett.

The Holliday Bookshop and the original Hamburger Heaven chain are gone, but today hamburger bars sprout up all over New York, and even the old Hamburger Heaven chain remains, under a different name, a pale, sad reminder of its suave old self. Today the ne plus ultra of the genre, at Daniel Boulud's DB Bistro Moderne, has become a tourist attraction. This ziggurat of prime sirloin, foie gras, and short ribs is a cinch to make yourself if you have a kitchen crew to bake the buns, bone and shred short ribs, combine them with foie gras and black truffles, and add these ingredients to the best sirloin, which is chopped, then roasted and placed on a bun sprinkled with Parmesan cheese, toasted and layered with tomato confit and a horseradish mayonnaise. Then all you have to do is add tomato and frisée and serve with pommes soufflées.

For years I would drive past McDonald's on the way

to Sag Harbor, noticing how many millions and then billions of their burgers had been sold. I was not surprised by these numbers, for McDonald's had stumbled upon an evolutionary defect in the human brain: an insatiable craving for fat and sugar on which primitive survival depended, a craving that has not moderated under civilized conditions, when fat and sugar have become an addictive menace and a marketing opportunity. McDonald's Pavlovian victims see the arches, respond to the primal need for energizing sugars and stored fat, and millions of stomachs, bypassing the brain, propel their owners toward them, oblivious to the risk of obesity and untimely death. McDonald's supplies enough calories from fat to sustain a daylong mammoth hunt and enough carbohydrates in its McNuggets, shakes, and fries for a quick sprint should one become the quarry. But with no more mammoths to hunt or saber-toothed tigers to run from, this unused energy simply adds to the gross weight of McDonald's billions of customers.

If hamburger addicts can control their appetites until they get home, they will save money and calories by buying fresh-ground sirloin or chuck with no more than 20 percent fat, forming it into quarter-pound burgers a half-inch thick, frying or grilling them over medium heat until just cooked through, and stuffing them into toasted supermarket buns with lettuce, tomato, onion, pickle, and whatever else their primal instincts demand. The burger itself may not be much less caloric than a Mac, but the home cook is unlikely to add fries and a sugary shake.

I patronize a quality butcher who trims his own prime beef and grinds the scraps for hamburger, which he sells for only slightly more than the supermarket charges for ground chuck.

PRIME BEEF HAMBURGER From the same shop I buy four-inch rolls and toast them lightly under the broiler. Then I shape the meat, which requires no seasoning, into six-ounce disks about three-quarters of an inch thick, grill them slowly in a ridged pan or beneath a slow broiler for four or five minutes per side, so that the outside doesn't burn before the inside cooks, and serve them just beyond medium rare—with only a trace of pink at the center—at which point the meat will be warmed through and won't crumble on the bun. Don't succumb to the temptation to squeeze the burgers with a spatula. Test them for doneness by pressing them lightly with a finger. The firmer they feel, the more they're done. I add a slice of sweet onion cut from the center and serve ketchup—sparingly, for it is full of corn sweetener—on the side. That my prime-beef hamburgers are less dangerous than Macnamara's is small consolation for the fact that I am no longer fourteen, beside a lake in Maine at dusk, with my friends at an outdoor counter under a string of colored bulbs, listening to Artie Shaw and the hum of crickets.

THREE

SUMMER
SCHOOL

Later, during college summers, I cooked in a restaurant on Cape Cod, drawn to that gritty work, I suspect, in preference to languid teenage days at Craigville Beach with friends, by memories of those aromatic mornings beside my grandmother's stove in Maine. One morning I made breakfast for a troupe of actors on their way to the playhouse at Dennis. A waitress told me that one of them was Gertrude Lawrence, but I had never heard of her and had no way of knowing whether or not it was she who had eaten my bright-yellow scrambled eggs, which I had beaten and cooked slowly in a buttered pan over hot water. I served the eggs with bacon, grilled flat and crisp under a weight, with a sprig of thyme, accompanied by one of my own blueberry muffins. Since I have been scrambling eggs over low heat for years, I must assume it was a kitchen colleague that summer who taught me to strain very fresh beaten eggs and scramble them over an improvised bain-marie rather than an open flame. **Now**

SCRAMBLED EGGS AND OMELETTES I use a Teflon sauté pan over a pot of simmering water and stir the amazing eggs from Iacono's farm on Long Lane in East Hampton with the back of a fork until the small curds mound up bright yellow and just firm. Usually I serve them simply scrambled, but with two or three shoves of the fork I sometimes roll them up as omelettes, holding the rolled omelette in the tilted pan over a high flame just long enough to brown the surface slightly, but leaving the inside slightly undercooked, before rolling it onto a warm plate and glazing it with butter from the pan. When I'm in the mood, I fill the omelettes with salmon roe or bits of smoked salmon or a few poached oysters. I no longer make and cannot recommend Devon Frederick's buttery, sugary, irresistible blueberry muffins, each one a day's worth of calories, but intrepid muffin fans will find a good approximation in the *Gold and Fizdale Cookbook,* now out of print but available secondhand.

My first restaurant assignment was the hot-dog-and-hamburger grill. The owner advertised that these were broiled in "creamery butter." They were not: they were fried in rendered beef fat, dyed yellow and packed in cardboard tubs marked "Stearin," probably the same lethal stuff that the big hamburger chains were using until recently for their fries. I was told to keep a brick of "butter" beside the grill, where the customers could see it. I did not feel good about this deception, but butter was scarce in that postwar summer, the owner wanted his "butter" on display, and I liked my job.

Restaurant cooks in those days were nothing like today's celebrities. Most of them, especially those who worked in seasonal resort towns, were drifters, who may have learned their trade at sea or in the service or prison. I liked to watch them dice vegetables fast and with precision, scoop them into a sauté pan, then, without looking, flip them and let them fall flawlessly back into the pan. These itinerant cooks tended to be childishly touchy and thought nothing of walking out on a busy weekend if their feelings were hurt or if they heard of a better job or got drunk. That first postwar summer, the kitchen was run by a rawboned, red-faced father-and-son team wearing identical red baseball caps. The son, who spoke Spanish, resented my status as a Columbia College freshman and called me the *perro-caliente* professor. The loquacious father told me about a one-legged hotel chef from Newark, New Jersey, who proved that oil floats on water by soaking his hands in ice water and then plunging them into hot oil without hurting himself, an improbable story but a useful demonstration that wet ingredients won't caramelize in hot oil because oil floats on water, so that the oil doesn't touch the food, which steams rather than browns. He and his taciturn son made their own potato chips, which they called Saratogas: russet potatoes sliced almost paper-thin on a mandoline, soaked briefly in water to get rid of the starch so that they wouldn't stick together as they fried, then drained and thoroughly dried in the cooler before they were plunged into hot oil. When I make these at home, I sometimes think of George's hands and wonder, against all reason, if that story could possibly have been true. Nevertheless, the fact that oil floats on water is an important lesson for deep-frying and caramelizing generally, and especially for salads. Unless you are using an oily emulsion or the greens are bone dry, add oil to the greens first, vinegar second, or both oil and vinegar will end up at the bottom of the salad bowl.

One night the red hats drifted away in the middle of dinner when the owner, having told them to stop stealing Four Roses from the bar, found them drinking his vanilla extract instead. They retaliated before they vanished by stuffing four boned loins of black-market beef into two ice-cream freezers, where the meat froze solid and could not be removed through the round openings. Rather than dismantle the freezers, the owner defrosted them, so that after two days the tops were turning green while the rest of the meat remained stuck. Only then did he dismantle the freezers. When he insisted on making hamburger from this mess, I quit, but was lured back with a new job as fry cook a week later, after he had thrown the spoiled meat away.

POTATO CHIPS You can make excellent potato chips at home in a domestic electric deep-fryer, but I use an old-fashioned fry pot with a long-handled wire basket, sold in restaurant-supply stores. Whichever you use, you will also need a mandoline or a similar device for cutting the chips. It is impossible to cut them thin enough by hand. If you are using an electric fryer, follow the manufacturer's instructions. Otherwise, pour about three inches of corn, soy, or canola oil—any of them will do, though canola is said to be less harmful—into a stovetop fry pot with a basket. Then peel four russet potatoes and trim the ends and sides to fit the carriage of your mandoline. Adjust your blade so that your potato slices are almost transparently thin but not so thin as to collapse in the oil. Then put the potato slices into a bowl of cold water to remove the starch so that the slices won't adhere as they fry. Meanwhile, heat the oil to 350 degrees. As the oil heats, drain the potato slices and spin them a handful at a time in a salad spinner. Finally, pat them dry with paper towels. If you have time, chill the slices in the refrigerator for an hour or so, until they are dry to the touch. Because oil floats on water, the drier the potatoes, the more they will be exposed to the oil, the faster they will brown, and the less your oil will bubble up when wet potatoes hit the hot oil. Add a few slices to test the oil. The potatoes should rise to the surface, where the oil will bubble gently as the chips brown. As soon as they have browned slightly and become crisp—you can feel the crispness with a wooden spoon or chopstick—remove them with a slotted spoon or Chinese strainer and drain them on paper towels. Do not overcook them or they will darken and become bitter. Salt them lightly. If the chips clump together in the oil as they brown, separate them gently with tongs or a chopstick. Then add the rest of the slices, a dozen or so at a time, adjusting the flame to compensate for the drop in temperature as you add each batch. I keep a sheet pan with some crumpled paper towels beside the fry pot on the stovetop and simply dump the fried chips from the basket onto the pan to drain.

You may prefer to adjust the shredding blade of your mandoline to cut the potatoes into matchsticks rather than chips. Rinse, dry, and fry as above. Chips and matchsticks, unlike conventional fries, remain crisp for days, look better on the plate, are less starchy, and in my opinion taste better, since they offer more crunchy surface and almost no mushy interior.

For a potato cake, peel and shred three pounds of all-purpose potatoes on the coarse side of a four-sided grater, then vigorously twist the shredded potatoes in a clean white towel to squeeze the water out. Barely film a nine-inch steel or well-seasoned cast-iron pan with vegetable oil. Heat the oil almost to smoking, then, with tongs and a spat-

HOT OIL Hot oil is dangerous. If you are using a stovetop fry pot and basket, put the handles where you can't inadvertently bump into them. Oil is slippery, so if you spill some on the floor, wipe it up at once. If you splash some on your hand, rinse it off with cold water, then dry your hands and apply cortisone cream. If the oil begins to smoke, lower the flame at once. If it catches fire, cover the pot until the flame subsides. DO NOT USE WATER! Use a fire extinguisher if necessary. Let used oil cool, then pour it into an empty tin and throw it out or strain it and use it in your diesel. Do not pour hot oil down the sink. It will melt the PVC drains.

POTATO CAKE ula, pile the potatoes neatly in the pan or skillet, forming a cake about a half-inch thick. The potatoes will shrink as their water evaporates. Shake the pan once or twice to loosen the potato cake; lower the flame so that the bottom won't burn before the center cooks. Loosen the bottom, if necessary, with a spatula. When the bottom forms a brown crust, and before it blackens, remove the pan from the flame, hold a plate tightly over the potatoes, and invert the pan, pouring off any excess oil. Then replace the potatoes in the pan, brown side up, and brown the other side slowly, to be sure the inside cooks. If all goes well, the outside will be crisp and the inside creamy. You can add snipped chives, green onion, grated nutmeg, salt, pepper, and/or whatever else pleases you to the shredded potatoes before you cook them.

There are lots of other ways to fry potatoes as cakes or hash browns—for example, by using day-old mashed or baked potatoes, or raw potatoes shredded on a mandoline or diced, but the basic procedure is the same. Unless they have already been mashed or baked and are therefore dry, remove as much water as possible, heat a little oil or butter or a combination in a smooth pan, and cook them slowly with your choice of extras. Then turn them over and brown the other side. For hash browns, don't form a cake but hash them up, flipping or tossing them with a spatula as they brown.

The restaurant where I worked that summer was an ambitious Howard Johnson franchise with a full dining room, table linens, and a bar opening onto an outdoor dance floor under a canopy with live music on weekends. That first postwar summer, I came of age, believing along with everyone else that we had won the war to end all wars and looking forward to a peaceful future in the best of all possible countries under the world's wisest rulers. I had learned the rudiments of a craft that I have never forgotten and, even more important, learned to respect the skills and the wisdom of my fellow workers—even those who plundered the boss's bar—who showed me, in the days when stainless steel couldn't hold an edge, how to care for my carbon-steel knives, which would turn black at the merest hint of acid and rusted in the humid kitchen. I learned that summer to make emulsions, to reduce veal stock for demi-glace, to sear and sauté fish and meat without having it stick in the days before Teflon, to use arrowroot to keep a blueberry pie from leaking without making it gummy, and to test a steak for doneness with my thumb until, by the end of summer, I could tell just by looking when a steak was rare, medium, or well. At midnight, after work, the cooks and waitresses would drive down with a case of beer to the stone breakwater at Hyannisport to cool off, and when the nights were too hot for us to sleep indoors we would spend the night on the flat rocks until awakened by the dawn. I also fell in love that summer, with a witty girl whose picture was on the cover of the August issue of the *Woman's Home Companion,* and wonder still from time to time what became of her.

FOUR

LUNCH IN
A WORLD TURNED
UPSIDE DOWN

For much of my life, I worked in the book-publishing business, mostly as editorial director at Random House, content to let others do the writing while I served them as banker, midwife, valet, and press agent. I also published a number of cookbooks by famous chefs and wrote several articles on cooking for various magazines. This probably explains why my friend Billy Norwich, who was working at *The New York Times*, called me in the summer of 2002 and asked if I could write a food column appropriate to the first anniversary of 9/11 for the Style Supplement of the *Times Magazine*. New York was still in pain from the attack, and Billy did not have to explain that his readers needed encouragement rather than another batch of recipes for autumn vegetables or turkey stuffing for the fall holidays.

I was intrigued by this assignment, and as I wondered

how to approach it, I remembered that the late food writer M. F. K. Fisher had in her twenties written bravely about food during a similarly grim period, midway through the 1930s in Europe, when the so-called civilized world was working itself up once again into a paroxysm of self-destruction and she was caught in the gathering chaos. So I thought it might interest readers of the *Times* on the first anniversary of 9/11 to learn how Fisher confronted her own world as it prepared to destroy itself. The volume called *The Gastronomical Me,* in which she collected her culinary reminiscences during these years, is preceded by this little prayer borrowed from a man named J. T. Pettee: "Pray for peace and grace and spiritual food, for wisdom and guidance, for all these are good, but don't forget the potatoes."

In 1936, Fisher was living in Dijon. She had tired of her professor husband and dreaded the prospect of afternoons back in the United States in a brown satin dress nibbling marshmallow salad with other faculty wives. She had, moreover, fallen head over heels in love with a man named Dillwyn Parrish, an American writer and artist. In her book she discreetly calls him Chexbres, Basque for "goat," revealing his actual identity only much later, in a memoir toward the end of her life. From Dijon they came to earth in Vevey, where they rebuilt an old farmhouse, from whose terrace they had a clear view across Lake Geneva to the mountains. But "when the terrace was too cool or breezy we set a long

French table in front of the open French windows and if the Lake seemed too wide and the Alps too high we could look into the great mirror opposite and make them more remote, less questioning of us." This is the essential Fisher, for whom the Alps must accommodate her when she and her lover sit down to lunch.

Their house had red tile floors, gardens, and good food. "In the summer there were always a lot of people: Vevey was on the road to almost any place in Europe and Le Paquis was such a pleasant little stop," she wrote, referring to their house. "Sometimes there were complications, political, national, religious, even racial but in general we managed to segregate the more violent prejudices. Once Chexbres had taken three socialists who were on their way to join the Spanish Loyalists to Cully for filet of perch while I served supper at Le Paquis to several charming but rabid Fascists from Rome, one of them a priest and all of them convinced that Communists were their personal as well as national enemies."

But it is not the twittering fascists who hold the reader's attention: it is the unseen Loyalist volunteers eating perch with Chexbres on their way to fight and perhaps be killed by fascists in Spain, a prospect that Fisher leaves to the reader's imagination. Earlier in that terrible year of Depression and war, she, her mother, and Chexbres had returned to Europe on the German vessel *Hansa,* "a tidy, plump little ship." "There was something comfortable about her, and at the same time subtly coarse and vulgar," an ugliness that was "part of what is happening now in the world . . . while men stunt their souls," Fisher wrote presciently in 1937, when few could yet grasp the unspeakable ugliness to come even as the men stood up in the ship's dining room "and lifted their glasses to the picture of Hitler at one end of the room." At night in her "clean and cozy" stateroom with "light shining on the cherry-satin feather-puff and the gleaming sheets," she would lock the door against evil and "the sickness and terror of the *Hansa*'s homeland." She wrote, "There was always a little silver tray in my cabin at night: thin sandwiches of rare beef, a pepper mill, a tiny bottle of cold champagne." In the morning, she would meet Chexbres for a twelve o'clock beer in the bar, and so they fell in love.

The most poignant of Fisher's memories of this period begins with sentences worthy of Isak Dinesen which could not have been written better by Hemingway that year. "There was a train, not a particularly good one, that stopped at Vevey about ten in the morning on the way to Italy. Chexbres and I used to take it to Milano. It had a restaurant car, an old-fashioned one with the agreeable austerity of a third-class station café about it: brown wooden walls and seats, bare tables unless you ordered the highest-priced lunch, and a few faded advertisements for Aspirina Bayer and '*Visitez le Maroc*' permanently crooked above the windows. There was one table, next to the galley, where the cooks and waiters sat. In the morning they would be talking and sorting greens for salad and cutting the tops off radishes."

It is the summer of 1939. Everyone knows that war is now inevitable. Chexbres had been gassed in the 1914 war and is dying. A leg has been amputated. Soon the other will have to go, Fisher coolly, lovingly reports. They have returned to Vevey for the last time and are now on their way to Milano. The waiters in the restaurant car, the old one with the patched jacket and the young one who had been trimming radishes, had grown fond of Fisher and her lover on previous trips. They try to hide their dismay at Chexbres's condition, but their solicitude betrays them as they hustle him and Fisher into the restaurant car early to spare them the company of the "Strength-through-Joyers"—coarse German tourists—who have squeezed into their compartment. When lunch is over, and the train is stopped at the border much longer than usual, the waiters invent pretexts to keep them at the table lest they discover the reason for the delay. A prisoner who had been taken aboard in chains that morning and led past their table in the restaurant car by two fascist agents has committed suicide by smashing the vestibule glass at the far end of the restaurant car and slitting his throat on the broken pane. The lovers know nothing of this, but when the train moves on into Italy at last, and they return to their compartment, they notice the broken pane and a dampness on the vestibule floor that had not been there before and they remember the man in chains being taken back to Italy.

That winter, their lives "had ended . . . with Chexbres' illness. And when we got word that we should go back to our old home in Switzerland and save what we could . . . we went, not so much for salvage, because possessions had no meaning any more to us, but because we were helpless to do anything else. We returned to the life that had been so real like fog, or smoke, caught in a current of air. We were very live ghosts, and drank and ate and saw and felt and made love better than ever before, with an intensity that seemed to detach us utterly from life."

By "life" she meant the life around them, for people "that summer, were laughing and singing and drinking wine in a kind of catalepsy, or like cancerous patients made happy with a magic combination of opiate before going into the operating theatre. We had finished with all that business, and they had it still to go through."

When I wrote about Fisher for the *Times,* its food page consisted of several introductory paragraphs and a few recipes, conventionally formatted. Had Fisher described some of the meals that she and Chexbres enjoyed, I would have tried to reconstruct them for the *Times*'s readers, but she didn't. Instead, I described the first lunch I managed to put together after 9/11, when, after two weeks confined to the wounded city with the smell of fire and death still clinging to our neighborhood, a mile or so north of where the Twin Towers had stood, it was time to drive out to Sag Harbor. I did so in low spirits, for the United States had been hurt and the new administration was untried. Judy, a foreign correspondent with years of experience in the Middle East, knew at once that the attack was the work of Islamic terrorists linked to those who had tried unsuccessfully to destroy the Towers eight years previously. The media were comparing the new attack to Pearl Harbor. But this seemed wrong. Japan had been a powerful nation. For FDR in 1941, war was the only possible response. But Osama bin Laden, who had by now emerged as the likely mastermind, was a gangster, a fanatic with religious pretensions, as Judy, who had been the first journalist to write about him at length, had written in the *Times*. As I drove out to Long Island that day, I wondered whether the shoot-from-the-hip Texan in the White House who had failed to anticipate the World Trade Center disaster—which, in retrospect, should have been foreseen—would be competent to prevent further attacks.

The Twin Towers had formed the backdrop to the cityscape that I see from my terrace, and though I found them intrusive and ugly as architecture, on foggy nights they glowed pleasantly, like candles through the mist. On that awful late-summer morning, under clear skies, I watched them burn, and for days we wore gauze masks when we went out. Those who could, left town. When I paid my weekly visit a few days later to Russ & Daughters, the century-old appetizer shop on Houston Street, I had to pass through a police checkpoint on my way home, where the officers, respectful of my age, did not bother to inspect my package of smoked salmon and herring. Instead, they offered to carry my bundle. The attack had rattled our confidence but made us a community. The streets were nearly empty that week and the next, except for police and street cleaners and heavy trucks rumbling north with debris. Our firehouse on Lafayette Street was banked with flowers and photographs of the men who had died, men whom I recognized and whose job had been to save our lives. I assumed that Bin Laden and his gang would be quickly captured. It never entered my mind that a year later he would still be at large while the United States would be at war with Iraq, which had nothing to do with the attack.

In Sag Harbor, near the eastern end of Long Island, a hundred miles or so from lower Manhattan, the Atlantic breeze was, as always after the long drive from the city, crisp and clean and exciting to breathe. I hadn't cooked since the eleventh and looked forward to feeding some friends who were coming down from Connecticut to stay with us for the weekend. So, before we turned off the highway toward Sag Harbor, I stopped at the Seafood Shop in the village of Wainscott to see what I could find for their lunch. What I found were some fillets of striped bass caught that morning, oysters from Fishers Island, and a bunch of cilantro. I also bought a two-pound lobster, a dozen hot-dog rolls—top-sliced, not side-sliced—and celery. Whatever else I needed was at home. Then we drove over to the airport to await our friends.

OYSTERS RAW AND FRIED

I opened two dozen oysters and served them with a half-glass of malt vinegar to which I added some chopped shallot and cracked black pepper. I also shucked another dozen oysters and dredged them in fine cornstarch mixed with a little Wondra flour, shook off the excess, and fried them in olive oil for no more than two minutes, until they were crisp and light brown, then served them on oyster shells into which I had spooned a dab of homemade mayonnaise thinned with lemon juice, a hint of hot sauce, and a sprinkling of minced chives from the garden.

WARM BASS SALAD

I also made a warm salad. I discarded the skin from a pound and a half of wild (not farmed) striped-bass fillet, cut the fish into one-inch cubes, removing the few small bones that remained, and dropped the cubed bass into a four-quart pot of gently boiling salted water, to which I had added a cup of white wine and half a lemon. I poached the fish just long enough so that I could break the cubes apart with a fork to the consistency of lump crabmeat. Timing here is crucial: Bass dries out quickly in poaching liquid. On the other hand, the bass has to be cooked through. So be careful. After about four or five minutes, I tested the bass with a small knife, and it was ready. I drained the cubes, dropped them into a colander, and broke them up. A few pieces were raw at the center, and I returned them to the pot for another minute. With the fish still warm in the colander, I napped it lightly with extra-virgin olive oil, lemon juice, and sea salt, and turned it all gently with a wooden spoon while continuing to let it drain. Then I tossed the warm bass with its dressing in a bowl with a good handful of chopped cilantro and tasted it for balance, adding whatever seemed necessary. I served this at once with a few Niçoise olives and a Pouilly-Fumé. Check the salad for salt before you serve it, taking care not to add too much. You might serve the salad with a few trimmed and quartered hearts of romaine, tossed in extra-virgin oil and showered with fresh-ground black pepper.

LOBSTER ROLLS I had already poached and chilled the two-pound lobster and removed the meat from the tail and claws, which I cut into roughly half-inch cubes. I mixed it with Hellmann's mayonnaise for the authentic Maine-coast lobster-shack taste, and two stalks of celery chopped not too fine so as to lose its crunch and sweetness but not so large as to distract from the lobster meat. Then I covered the bowl and left it in the refrigerator to chill.

After I had served the warm bass salad and removed the yellow plates with the blue fleur-de-lis that my son, Jacob, and his wife, Susie, had sent from California, I melted two tablespoons or so of butter in an iron skillet large enough to hold four top-sliced hot-dog rolls. When the butter stopped bubbling, I added the rolls and cooked them until they had browned slightly—barely a minute on each side— being careful not to let them burn in the hot butter. Then, holding each hot roll in a kitchen towel with one hand and a pair of tongs in the other, I piled the chilled salad into the hot rolls almost to overflowing, sprinkling the tops with a pinch of paprika. Lobster rolls have lately become popular in New York restaurants, but they are not always successful. Too often the meat is cut or even ground into small dice or shreds, resulting in a watery, flavorless salad served at room temperature or, in one egregious case, served warm, whereas the classic preparation calls for substantial, slightly chilled chunks, too large to leak and become watery, contrasting with the warm roll, whose toasted sweetness combines wonderfully with the different sweetness of the chilled lobster in its Hellmann's dressing.

FIVE

A BACKWARD
GLANCE

L ong Island, whose clean waters supplied our lunch, stretches some 130 miles at exactly ninety degrees from New York City, ending in a split tail, its flukes known locally as the North and South Forks. Walt Whitman, who was born on the Island, compared it to a whale, its blunt head pressed up against Manhattan to the west and its forked tail marking the entrance to Long Island Sound. If you look at a map, you will see at once what he meant. Of the two forks, the South has always been the more prosperous, and with the coming of the railroad from New York in the 1890s, the more fashionable as well. The prosperity is the result of the retreating glacier at the end of the last ice age, some ten or twelve thousand years ago, when the melting ice exposed the rich compost amassed as the glacier, like a giant push broom, scraped its way south from what is now New England to the sea. The terminal moraine, a ridge which marks the southernmost reach of the glacier, runs down the spine of the South Fork from east to west. The outwash plain of rich topsoil sloping down from the moraine to the sea—even today, after nearly four centuries of aggressive cultivation—produces miracles summer after summer. You can stand on the beach and see the thick layer of black soil where it has been eroded by the sea, sandwiched between its top layer of grass and bottom layer of white sand.

The rich soil and the even richer whale fishery, oyster beds, and waters teeming with finfish, lobster, and crab, to say nothing of waterfowl, must have seemed like paradise to the Kentish settlers of the South Fork in the seventeenth century. The bounty shipped by these settlers to the Indies from the port of Sag Harbor, where I live in an old Federal house surrounded by trimmed boxwood and old perennial gardens, made them rich. They named their villages after the English places from which they had come: Riverhead, Wainscott, Southampton, Maidstone (which the Americans changed to East Hampton after the Revolution; amid Sag Harbor's old houses this can still seem like a recent event). Some descendants of these early settlers still live and farm here. But it was the railroad speculators, promising their hapless investors that Montauk, the fishing village at the tip of the South Fork, would become the western terminus of transatlantic sea routes, who brought the train to eastern Long Island, and with it New York's summertime plutocracy, as well as many artists, from Thomas Moran to Willem de Kooning, drawn here by the company of their fellow artists and by the tender light and air. The autumn pumpkins and the cornstalks, the long white stretch of beach against a green sea through a scrim of mist, the true red of a hefty September tomato still warm from the sun, the gleaming bass and the swordfish at the Seafood Shop are the scenery of my Long Island days, but even after forty years I don't feel quite real here, for the lakes and dark forests of Maine are the default landscape of my soul.

In 1912, the fantasy of a deepwater port at Montauk and a fast ride by rail into New York sank along with the *Titanic,* which had been rumored to inaugurate the long-awaited Montauk terminus. But by then the railroad had already made the South Fork of Long Island a fashionable resort, edged by miles of magnificent beachfront, part of the strand stretching from Montauk west to Coney Island, at the entrance to New York Harbor.

I have offered this brief history of Long Island to locate, for readers who may not be familiar with this part of the world, the old whaling port of Sag Harbor, which I consider my home, and which was settled three centuries ago as the sheltered, deepwater port for the prosperous towns of Southampton and Maidstone, before it became East Hampton. It was on a Sag Harbor whaler that Queequeg, Melville's Polynesian harpooner in *Moby-Dick,* stowed away, hoping to become a Christian and return to convert his royal Polynesian family. But after coming ashore at rowdy Sag Harbor, he decided to take a look at Nantucket, then chose to remain a pagan. This louche reputation lingered well into the twentieth century. As late as the 1970s, the *East Hampton Star* seldom referred to Sag Harbor without a condescending snicker. Though this fertile end of Long Island has now been wantonly overdeveloped, there is still enough protected farmland left to supply the surviving hedge-funders and investment bankers in their beachfront palaces with magnificent tomatoes, sweet corn, greens, peaches, and apples well into autumn, when the billionaires straggle south, leaving the gleanings of their summertime abundance to the Canada geese who strut across the abandoned golf courses and pick the harvested fields clean.

Sag Harbor, its old houses jammed side by side on crooked streets and occupied now mainly by writers, editors, and philosophers, has been spared this over-development, for there has been almost no open space here to build upon since the nineteenth century. For years following the decline of the whaling trade and the failure of all but a handful of industries, Sag Harbor fell silently into decrepitude, too poor even to demolish its fading old houses and commercial buildings. Most of these sturdy structures have now been artfully restored, so that visitors interested in vernacular styles of American domestic architecture will find here a living museum of Federal, Greek Revival, as well as a rare

Egyptian Revival church, Swiss Cottage, and other Victorian styles, inhabited not by bewigged actors in period costume but by actual dogs, people, and children.

A century ago, families would take the train out to Southampton for weekend duck dinners at John Duck's famous restaurant, a short walk from the depot. Never a favorite of the seasonal nobility, John Duck's was patronized by the local burghers and known not so much for its ducks, which were still roasted in their own fat rather than with the fat extruded in the current fashion, but for its addictive coleslaw, which was served as a kind of amuse-bouche. John Duck's is now out of business, but the composition of its coleslaw continues to intrigue local cooks.

One day last summer, at Halsey's farm stand in Watermill, as I waited to be served, I was wondering aloud to a friend whether to buy yet another cabbage and try once again to solve the mystery of John Duck's coleslaw. "I know the recipe," conspiratorially whispered the farm-stand proprietor, who had been following our conversation. "Wait here. I'll be right back." She darted away to her house to retrieve her recipe box. "Look through it," she said, "and you'll find it." And so I did.

John Duck used an old fashioned cabbage grinder that quickly and accurately reduced the vegetables to a confetti-like but still-crunchy texture. A carefully managed food processor produces similar results, batch by batch.

JOHN DUCK'S COLESLAW Remove the outer leaves and core from a medium head of green cabbage. Cut the cabbage in quarters, and each quarter in three chunks. Put as much as will fit easily in a food processor, and process off and on four or five times, until most of the cabbage has been ground to the size of confetti but no smaller. Empty the ground cabbage into a bowl, remove any large pieces, and add them to the next batch. Cut a bell pepper in chunks, and chop a carrot and two stalks of celery coarsely, and run them quickly through a food processor, retaining as much texture as possible. Cut an onion separately by hand into very small dice, but be careful not to add too much or it will overwhelm everything else. For a medium cabbage, mix one cup of mayonnaise—either Hellmann's, to save time, or homemade sweetened with a third of a cup of sugar and diluted with enough milk to melt the sugar and thin the mayonnaise without making it watery. Or substitute buttermilk or plain, unstrained yogurt for milk. Then mix all the ingredients with a teaspoon of caraway seed, add salt very carefully, a few grains at a time, and a few splashes of white vinegar to taste. Chill it for an hour or so. The result will be first cousin to John Duck's, but creamier and crunchier.

FRIED CHICKEN I like to serve this coleslaw with Sal Iacono's two-and-a-half-pound chickens, cut in eight pieces, which I marinate in Lawry's Seasoning for a few hours, dip lightly in flour or Wondra, shaking off the excess, and fry the drumsticks and thighs first, then the breasts and wings, in vegetable oil at 350 degrees in a cast-iron skillet, taking care that the oil is not so deep as to cover the chicken, which I turn several times, so that the skin does not blacken where it touches the pan. The chicken is done when the internal temperature reaches 135 degrees on an instant-read thermometer, after about ten minutes for the legs and thighs and a minute or two longer for the breasts. For three-and-a-half-pound chickens, the legs and thighs will take a little longer and the breasts not so long. Don't try this with factory-raised chickens. They will be dry and tasteless.

Sal Iacono, in his white apron and farmer's rubber boots, was an East Hampton institution; he died in 2008 at seventy-nine. His widow and son now carry on the business. Long before the term "free range" was invented, Sal's chickens were running this way and that outdoors in good weather in a half-acre pen, and when it rains they file two by two into their spacious henhouse. Since the 1950s, when he inherited the farm from his father, he had raised his chickens on a simple diet of corn without chemicals, hormones, antibiotics, or anything else in a clean henhouse, and he sold them the day after they were killed. The chickens are the widely grown Cornish Cross, so what gives them their intense flavor and delicate texture must be their diet of unadulterated grain, their freedom to wander outdoors in search of food, their freshness, and perhaps the clean East Hampton air—in other words, their freedom to live like other birds. Whatever the reason, they are unlike any other chickens I have ever tasted, including the celebrated blue-legged *poulets de Bresse* of France. Sal himself was as cheerful and easygoing as his chickens must have been to produce such flavor and texture, an honorable and humorous man, without pretense, who made a fine product, gave good value, enjoyed his work and his customers, and in his humble shop played tapes of the music to which he (and I) came of age many years ago.

Lately, Peconic Bay scallops, which used to grow in our bays like weeds, have been severely depleted by an invasion of algae. Now they seem to be returning, not yet in their former great numbers but enough to inspire hope that the worst is over, though another "brown tide" is moving ominously through the bays. These scallops are so sweet and tender that I like to eat them raw, lightly marinated in lime juice, with a few shreds of raw onion and some finely diced chilis. Most people, however, prefer them sautéed or fried.

FRIED SCALLOPS AND FRIED CALAMARI

To fry them I heat a half-inch of extra-virgin olive oil in a ten-inch cast-iron skillet until the oil begins to shimmer. Then I dredge a handful of scallops at a time in corn flour and discard any excess by tossing the scallops, a few at a time, in a colander, batting the colander firmly with my hand, and with tongs or a slotted spoon I lower the scallops carefully into the oil, so that the oil doesn't splash and the scallops don't gang up. They will brown quickly, and as soon as they do you must remove them from the oil and drain them on paper towels. Offer these to guests with drinks before dinner, three to a serving, with a wooden toothpick and a touch of cold mayonnaise thinned with lemon juice. Or serve them as a first course with andouille or chorizo sausage in small chunks warmed through in the same pan.

Sometimes I accompany fried scallops with fried calamari. I use the smaller ones, which I cut in quarter-inch rings, trimming the heads by cutting off the eyes. I dip them in milk and then in a mixture of Wondra flour and corn flour. After shaking off the excess, I fry them in olive oil at about 350 degrees for a minute or two, until they brown slightly. Then I drain them on paper towels, salt them, and serve them at once, while they are still crisp. They are much more delicate than the heavily breaded restaurant versions, but the delicate batter won't stay dry for long, so don't fry more at a time than your guests can eat in five minutes. Most fish markets sell squid already cleaned. If yours doesn't, simply separate the head and tentacles from the bodies, then remove the transparent cartilage from the body, remove the pinkish skin, rinse out the body, and proceed as above. Do not leave the calamari in the oil for more than a minute or two or they will become mushy. The aroma of squid frying in olive oil reminds me of seaside lunches at Amalfi. You may also grill very small calamari, bodies split lengthwise, flattened out, patted dry, and seared in a ridged grill pan, quickly, on high heat until the grill marks begin to appear.

FETTUCCINE WITH SCALLOPS

Another, rather rich way to serve bay scallops for six as a first course at dinner, or a main course at lunch, is simply to poach a pound of bay scallops in a stick of hot butter with a whole garlic clove, sprinkling them with a few leaves of finely chopped rosemary—just a hint, since rosemary is very strong. Meanwhile, boil a pound of fettuccine, preferably fresh, and when the pasta is al dente, lift it out with tongs or a pasta fork and add it to the scallops with half a cup of heavy cream, a cup of fresh-grated Parmesan, a few grains of sea salt, and a sprinkling of white pepper. This simple dish—essentially fettuccine Alfredo with scallops tinged with rosemary—is wonderfully comforting, especially for long-distance bicycle racers in need of carbohydrates. If the pasta seizes up, add a cup or so of pasta water.

FETTUCCINE WITH CLAMS Another version of this dish, which I learned from the late Pierre Franey, is to use shucked and chopped cherrystone clams instead of scallops, and add a good handful of chopped basil and some fresh-ground black pepper to the fettuccine, which I boil in water mixed with clam juice. I omit the Parmesan. This dish is so rich that I seldom make it now, but when I do I serve only a generous forkful in a large pasta bowl to each guest as a first course.

CLAMS CASINO I also like to serve as a canapé my version—there are countless others—of clams casino. For these you should ask the fishmonger for small cherrystone clams or largish littlenecks, which are called "top necks" on Long Island. You will need three or four per guest. If you can't open them yourself, ask the fishmonger to open them for you. Opening them is easy enough once you get used to it, but it takes some practice. You will need a clam knife. I prefer the kind with a somewhat flexible, thin blade. Don't use an ordinary knife. If you are right-handed, hold the clam in your left hand, against the thumb joint, using your thumb as a clamp. You will notice that the clam is shaped rather like an ear, tightly curled at the top. Look carefully for where the two shells join at the top of this ear. The point is to hold the blade of your clam knife in your right hand (again, if you are right-handed) vertically against this notch, which is not always easy to find, and press the blade with the fingers of your left hand firmly into the notch. Adjust the clam in your hand for maximum leverage. Once you have wedged the blade firmly between the shells, turn the blade ninety degrees and twist the shells apart. Then cut the muscle which attaches the clam to the top shell, and discard the top shell. Don't be discouraged if you don't succeed the first or even the fifth time. You will eventually get the hang of it. Another solution is simply to put the unopened clams in a dry pan in a medium oven for ten minutes or so, until they begin to open by themselves. Since you are going to put the clams under the broiler eventually, this unorthodox method won't substantially change the result, but you will not have had the pleasure of going mano a mano with a clam. If you plan to serve the clams raw, on the half-shell, and they don't open easily, put them on ice in your freezer for ten minutes or so, and then pry them open. Clam openers at raw bars use this trick.

For my version of two dozen clams casino, you will need a green bell pepper; a sweet onion; a small jar of pimientos or a red bell pepper blistered over a flame, skinned, and diced; a jalapeño; some lemon juice; a half-stick of softened unsalted butter; Worcestershire sauce; and four slices of bacon. Remove the top and bottom and scrape out the seeds from the bell pepper, and cut it into thin julienne strips. Then cut the strips into fine dice. Dice the onion similarly, and chop the pimiento or skinned red bell pepper. There should be roughly equal amounts of each vegetable. Mince the jalapeño extra-fine (no seeds), and add it to the mix. Now wash your hands, lest you inadvertently rub your eyes. Mash two tablespoons or so of softened butter, and an equal amount of Worcestershire, into the vegetable mix. Meanwhile, cut four slices of good bacon into twenty-four pieces and soften them in a pan over a medium flame. Mix a tablespoon of bacon fat into the filling, and place a generous pinch or two on each opened clam, topping each with the softened bacon. Place the clams on a broiler pan, and put them in the refrigerator until you are ready to heat and serve them. When ready to serve, put the clams under a medium broiler until the bacon is crisp but before it burns, and serve while hot. You may want to experiment a bit with the mix.

There are countless varieties of clams, but for practical purposes in the northeastern United States there are only two: hard-shell and soft-shell. Manilla clams, which I prefer for pasta with clam sauce, are imported from the West Coast. Hard-shell clams are the littlenecks (smallest), cherrystones (larger), and chowders or quahogs (pronounced "co-hogs"), the largest, found in most East Coast fish markets. They are eaten raw on the half-shell, or stuffed with oregano and bread crumbs and baked, or as clams casino (see above), or with pasta, though the much smaller manilla clams are more subtle and intense with pasta. Soft-shell clams are less often seen in New York markets but are common in New England, where they are steamed or fried. Hard-shell clams are also steamed, usually with a celery stalk and a sprinkle of chopped parsley, and the two varieties are interchangeable in chowders, but only soft-shell clams are fried. They are eaten raw only by seagulls.

FRIED SOFT-SHELL CLAMS
Soft-shells are easier to open than hard-shell clams, but their shells tend to crumble. This is a problem if you want to fry them, which requires that you shuck them first. But if you're careful, you can open them gently by trimming away the membrane that holds the top and bottom shells together and delicately cutting the muscle that holds the clam to its shell. Then remove and discard the black sheath covering the neck, and dip each clam in cool water to get rid of the sand. For frying, you should look for smaller clams, two inches or so from top to bottom. They are easier to eat. Save the larger ones for steaming. Dip the clams in buttermilk or condensed or plain milk and then toss them to coat in a mixture of one-third all-purpose wheat flour and two-thirds corn flour and a pinch of fine sea salt. In a colander, shake off the excess. The battered clams will become soggy unless they are fried at once. Drop them immediately, one by one, into a fry basket, and drop the basket into corn, peanut, or canola oil at 360 degrees, cooking for a minute or so, just until they are

the color of a paper bag. They will fry more quickly after the first batch. Drain them on paper towels. If I'm frying a lot of clams, I set a sheet pan on the stove beside my fry pot, line it with paper towels, and drop the fried clams on it. The classic accompaniment is tartar sauce made from a cup of Hellmann's mayonnaise, chopped pickle relish, a tablespoon of capers, drained, lemon juice, a little chopped onion or shallot, and a tablespoon of Dijon mustard.

So-called Ipswich clams are soft-shell clams dug mostly from the coastal mudflats north of Boston. The rich mud provides their unique sweetness, noticeably different from their bland cousins dug from sandy bottoms. But genuine Ipswich clams have been scarce lately, and most clams sold under that name are harvested from mudflats along the Maine coast. The shells of clams dug from mud tend to be darker than those dug from sand. Occasionally the Seafood Shop in Wainscott, Long Island, has these darker clams, and though they are a long way from Ipswich, their greater intensity is noticeable. My fried clams are much more delicate than the heavily battered, more durable version sold by roadside stands. They should be eaten while still warm. With fried squid, oysters, and whitebait, if you can find it, they make a great fritto misto.

STEAMED SOFT-SHELL CLAMS For steamed soft-shell clams, simply rinse the clams under the faucet to wash away the sand, and place the clams in a covered pot over a medium flame. In five minutes or so, the shells will have opened. Scoop up the clams from the pot with a Chinese strainer and drop them into a serving bowl. Strain the broth from the pot into as many mugs as you have guests, and serve each guest a small cup of melted butter. Guests should remove the clams from their shells and slip off and discard the black membrane from the neck. Then they should dip the clam into the broth to remove any remaining sand, and from there into the butter.

My mother, who needed no lessons in self-esteem, enjoyed, in her damp, drizzly November moods, taunting my father with the claim that she had agreed to their courtship only when he offered to treat her to fried Ipswich clams at Hugo's Lighthouse Restaurant on Boston's South Shore. Thus I learned at a vulnerable age that because of a fried clam I am. Perhaps this is why New York, where Ipswich clams are hard to find, still doesn't seem, after so many years, like home.

SIX

THE OWL AND THE PUSSYCAT
GO TO SEA IN A BEAUTIFUL
FRENCH LINE BOAT

On the morning of December 30, 1953, my first wife, Barbara, and I were married at a friend's apartment in Morningside Heights in upper Manhattan, adjacent to Columbia University, from which I had graduated in 1949, with no idea what to do with the rest of my life and in no hurry to find out. At Columbia my friends and I read and studied literature as a kind of religion, an inexhaustible source of wisdom, we believed, to which we became addicted: Plato, the unknown authors of Ecclesiastes and Job, Dante, Shakespeare, Cervantes, Gibbon, Tolstoy. I wanted only to read, and after graduation that's what I did that summer, at a lakeside cabin, alone in Oakland, Maine, with Proust, Balzac, and Gibbon and, at bedtime, Yeats, whose concern for the fragility of cultures and their artifacts I share. I was too much in awe of the writers I worshipped to think that I might become a writer myself, but after a pointless year in graduate school, I was ready to leave the academy. My favorite pre-Socratic philosopher, Heraclitus, said that character is fate: we become what we are. So, relying upon Heraclitus, I wandered into the book-publishing business and became a valet and evangelist for writers.

This unexpected vocation explains why Barbara and I were speeding, after our wedding, down Manhattan's West Side Highway, beside the sparkling Hudson, under a brilliant windswept sky, to the pier where the stately *Ile de France,* its old-fashioned perpendicular bows towering over the highway, was preparing to sail at noon. We had booked a first-class cabin. Neither of us had money, but two years previously I had suggested to the publishing company where I worked that, with the market for books bound to expand as a result of the GI Bill, the kinds of books my classmates were reading would sell many more copies as inexpensive but well-made paperbacks than as expensive hardcovers, which students could not afford. There was nothing new about my idea. European publishers had been publishing serious books in paperback, the kind I had in mind, for years. But in the United States at that time, paperback books, except for a few imported Penguins, were mostly ephemera sold in drugstores and at newsstands and removed at the end of each month along with that month's magazines, to be replaced with next month's thrillers, mysteries, and westerns. My plan to publish important books on good paper, slightly larger than drugstore paperbacks, and stock them permanently in bookstores, succeeded beyond anyone's expectations, including my own, and this voyage was my reward for having precipitated what came to be called the paperback revolution.

In those pre-jet days, when all but the most intrepid transatlantic travelers sailed to Europe, book publishers went first-class. Book publishing has never been a very profitable business. To make money, you went to work in a bank. Book publishing was a vocation. Without money you might go hungry. Without books you would not know who you are or where you came from or where you might be going. For me and many others, the work we did in those years was its own reward. The annual three-week scouting trip to England and the Continent by sea was a traditional perquisite. First-class passage was compensation for monastic wages. Barbara and I were going to meet the important postwar European writers. We were twenty-five and fearless. We would be gone not for the prescribed three weeks but for three months.

First-class passengers took an elevator to the upper level of a covered West Side pier and crossed a broad, red-carpeted gangplank onto the ship. There were confetti and streamers; bellboys in pillbox hats with chin straps, delivering bouquets; porters in berets and the insignia "CGT" in red concentric circles on their blue sweaters; pages shouting names and waving telegrams; chimes warning visitors that they would soon have to go ashore. Did I imagine it or did I see Van Johnson, the actor, a camel's-hair coat over his shoulders, retreating down the gangplank backward, waving? I remember the buttery aroma of fresh croissants, which I have ever since associated with that voyage. The *Ile de France* would prove to be a seagoing patisserie.

Our cabin was not large, but spacious enough not to be overwhelmed by its walls of silk brocade, the Louis XV chairs, or the pink silk lampshades. I have a photograph of Barbara in a gray suit, hat, and veil sitting on the arm of one of these chairs. I'm standing behind her. Barbara seems stunned. I'm smiling. My confidence was not ill-founded. Our generation of Americans had every reason to trust the future. Hitler and the Japanese, as we had never doubted, were defeated. The war in Korea was an anomaly and far away. The imperial troubles to come were not yet in sight. I had been rejected for the Korean draft when the examining doctor asked when I had had polio. I said never. He said, "Think again," and then I remembered my eighth or ninth summer, when I came down with a fever which my father said was the grippe. It had never occurred to me that this might have been polio, nor did my parents tell me. The doctor said that my right foot had been affected, something I had not previously noticed. Before I could dispute his diagnosis, I was asked to leave the line of candidates and go home. I disliked being rejected, but on reflection chose not to pursue the issue. Perhaps the doctor decided that the army would be better off without me. Our marriage proved bountiful.

Though after many years it ended, the love we cele-brated that day survives, undiminished after Barbara's death last year.

By the time we found our way to the cabin, our friends had already arrived to say goodbye and spilled out onto the corridor. I remember yellow orchids and champagne splits in a silver tub of ice, bits of conversa-tion. Then they left, and I was alone on the afterdeck looking down at the tugs as they backed the ship away from the pier and into the Hudson.

The next day was stormy. By late afternoon, the *Ile de France,* which had seemed so sturdy when its old-fashioned bows towered over the West Side Highway, was laboring through messy seas. Wrapped in blankets in a deck chair on the glassed-in promenade, I watched the ocean seem to rise almost to the level of the deck and then fall steeply away. Chopin and Satie drifted down from hidden speakers. Lunch, served on deck, had been chicken sandwiches, smoked salmon, and Chablis. I was reading the Maude translation of *War and Peace.* Edmund Wilson, the distinguished literary critic and essayist, was also aboard, with his wife, Elena. He was on his way to Israel to write about the Dead Sea Scrolls for *The New Yorker.* Wilson's abundant output in those years required the services of several publishers. I was one of them, and we had become friends. That evening, Edmund and Elena joined us at the New Year's Eve gala in the first-class dining room, with its grand double staircase and double-height ceiling. We had been assigned a table for six, and when the four of us arrived we found the great comic actor Buster Keaton and his wife in the other two seats. Keaton seemed uncomfortable in his tuxedo and old-fashioned starched collar. He barely spoke, oblivious to the pitching and rolling ship, unblinking, his mouth a horizontal slit, his eyes straight ahead, as deadpan as the character he played. He seemed to have no idea that Wilson in his world was as distinguished as himself in his. But when Wilson, a gifted prestidigitator who was juggling several festive cotton balls handed out at ships' galas in those days, suggested to Keaton that he might perform for the passengers, Keaton replied politely but without expression, "No props," and silently began juggling some cotton balls himself. I remember crêpes Suzette and cherries jubilee aflame as waiters struggled to remain upright beneath their trays, amid fox-trotters sliding this way and that across the polished floor, as the ship rose and fell through violent seas. "No props," indeed.

In Paris, we lived in a vast, gloomy apartment at 35 rue de la Faisanderie, off Avenue Foch, looked after by an ancient housekeeper who replied to our infrequent requests, *"J' vais au cimetière."* Someone had told us that the Grand Véfour, in the Palais Royal, was the best restaurant in Paris, so almost every day Barbara and I went there for lunch or dinner or both. With American money, everything was cheap, even the best three-star restaurants. On the ship we had drunk La Tâche for five dollars a bottle. The Grand Véfour, which had opened in 1784 as Café de Chartres, is still the most beautiful dining room in Paris, with its gilt mirrors and red velvet upholstery. The menu was classic: quenelles de brochet, sole Véronique, coulibiac Colette (named for the great writer, who lived in the Palais Royal and took her meals occasionally in the Grand Véfour, but whom we never had the good fortune to see). One day at lunch, we were each offered an ortolan, the tiny bunting that is fattened and roasted to be swallowed whole, a delicacy in southwestern France since before Caesar crossed the Rubicon. These birds were then and may still be an endangered species, and could not be served legally, but we had become regulars, and this illicit treat was the manager's way of welcoming us.

When we tired of the Grand Véfour, we tried more modest places: Lapérouse, with its *cabinets particuliers,* and Chez Allard, in the Sixth, with its rustic menu. It was there that I first had braised duck with olives, one of the few Parisian dishes of the expiring Escoffier period not covered with béchamel or espagnole in various forms. For years I served my version of this classic dish at home in New York, and occasionally still do.

From Paris we flew to Berlin, which by then had begun to dig itself out of its wartime rubble. Bricks from ruined buildings were piled neatly along the Kurfürstendamm. The cabarets were open all night. But politically Berlin seemed to be digging itself back in, for the Cold War had begun, and Berlin, deep within the Soviet sector, was its central front. The best bookstore with fine editions of Russian classics was in the Soviet zone, and so was the best restaurant. It served thick soups, black bread, sausages, and fried potatoes in many versions. For years I kept the menu in my desk. In the United States there were no collected editions of our classic writers, an omission which, at the suggestion of Edmund Wilson, I would eventually correct. Some writers whom we met in the American zone who were working for the CIA warned us to avoid the Russian zone. The Cold War ground rules had yet to be clarified, and there was talk of kidnappings. We ignored this advice and returned often for soup and sausages, reluctant to admit that, with the war so recently ended, we were preparing to go at it again. In Berlin, amid our Cold War friends, Korea was no longer an anomaly. War now seemed routine, accompanied by the ideological quarrels in the intellectual journals that I now found it obligatory to read, and which would soon convince me that warfare, both cold and hot, is our normal state, and peace an aberration.

We were happy to leave this bleak city still largely in ruins and drift off to Italy for a few weeks. We had been away too long and were ready to think about going home. I wondered whether I still had a job after my long absence.

We arranged passage on the *Andrea Doria* from Naples. In the Azores, the cheerful little ship became fogbound. We arrived in port a day late. Our waiter, whose glasses had broken during the crossing and hung lopsided across his Roman nose, explained that because of the delay we had run out of pasta. On deck as we approached our pier, an Italian father was holding his two small sons in his arms, pointing to the Manhattan skyline, and shouting, *"Fantastico, bambini, fantastico."* Despite the warlike rumblings in Berlin, this was how it seemed to us, too, in the early spring of 1954. In my absence, the paperback series I had launched had gone from triumph to triumph. I was welcomed back, enthusiastically.

Barbara and I were relieved to be back in our Greenwich Village garret, which after our month in Paris seemed to us more than ever like a set from *La Bohème* with its skylight and fireplace, its old brick walls, crooked floor, and window boxes filled with geraniums in spring. We had spent the last three months in hotels and restaurants and other people's dining rooms. I was eager to cook at home, but not like our favorite Grand Véfour with its Escoffier menu. It was obvious to us that the mood had shifted. In the Paris bookshops, stacks of Samuel Beckett's plays were piled up everywhere, and there was an existentialist on every street corner. In London, still aching from the war, *The Waste Land* was on everyone's lips, with intimations of *A Clockwork Orange* just ahead. Inevitably, an "existential" cuisine was not far off. It would take many forms, from the Zen bakeries of San Francisco to the innovations of *la nouvelle cuisine* with its deconstruction of culinary metaphysics. It was in this spirit that I began to reproduce some of the simpler dishes we had encountered on our trip. Chez Allard's wonderfully simple braised duck with olives became a favorite.

BRAISED DUCK WITH OLIVES

Nothing is easier than braising a duck and serving it with olives. You will need a heavy nonreactive Dutch oven, preferably porcelain over cast iron, a three-and-a-half-to-four-pound Pekin duck, a little oil for browning the duck, thyme and rosemary for stuffing, assorted vegetables, a half-bottle of Pinot Noir, port, arrowroot to thicken the braising liquid, a little Cognac, and some pitted picholine or similar olives. Dry the duck with paper towels, and with a hair dryer if you happen to have one. Remove the loose fat from neck and tail, prick the skin all over with a fork, and season the inside with salt and pepper, then stuff the duck with a few branches of rosemary and thyme. The skin should be very dry in order to brown evenly. Remove and save the wings. Heat a little oil or rendered duck fat in the Dutch oven, and brown the duck, breast side down at first, then the back and sides. When the duck is nicely browned, lift it from the cocotte, set it aside, and pour off all but a few tablespoons of fat. Toss in the duck neck, wings, and giblets (but not the liver), an onion studded with a few cloves, two medium carrots, chopped, and two stalks of celery, diced, the juice and zest of half a lemon, and two or three bay leaves. Brown the giblets and wings and caramelize the vegetables in the duck fat left in the pot. Then blend a tablespoon of arrowroot or Wondra instant-blending flour into the vegetables to make a roux, and cook for a minute or so. Heat and add to the pot two cups of rich chicken or duck stock with a cup of port and three cups of Pinot Noir or similar robust red wine. Turn the flame to high and reduce the wines and stock by a third. The liquid should not cover the duck when you return it to the cocotte, breast side down, resting on the wings, which serve as a kind of couch. Add a good pinch of sea salt. Cover the cocotte with plastic wrap, place the lid on top, and braise the duck slowly in a 325-degree oven for about an hour, checking occasionally that the breast isn't scorched, until the leg meat is firm and the breast runs yellow when pierced. Strain the stock, discard the wings and giblets, and press the vegetables to extract the liquid. Pour the liquid into a clear glass container. Let it cool, and spoon off as much fat as possible. Or use a fat separator with a spout at the bottom and pour off the clear liquid. Better yet, chill the liquid for an hour or so, until the fat congeals enough to be spooned completely away. Reduce the stock to the consistency of light cream. If it's too thick, thin it with a little chicken or duck stock. If it's too thin, boil it down more. Add to the stock a handful of pitted picholine or similar green or black pitted olives. Heat a half-cup of cognac, add it to the stock, and flame it. When the duck is cool enough to handle, remove the breast meat with the grain in long, rather thin slices. Remove the legs at the joint and trim them neatly, removing any loose fat. Then arrange the legs with the sliced breast meat nicely on a warm platter. Nap with the warm sauce and olives, and serve. A Lynch-Bages from a good year would be just right, or a fine American Pinot Noir.

PURÉED RUTABAGA Autumn rutabaga—peeled, hacked in chunks, and boiled until tender, then puréed with butter and a little salt in a food processor—would be a perfect accompaniment; or, more elegantly, pass the softened rutabaga through a food mill, then add butter and salt. Grilled Treviso radicchio or endive, a lightly curried cauliflower purée, or turnips in wedges braised in duck fat are also fine accompaniments.

Save the duck fat, which is said to be less harmful than other animal fats. Add a tablespoon of duck fat to a pound of lean chuck to make a poor man's version of Daniel Boulud's hamburgers with foie gras.

There are many kinds of ducks, and many ways to prepare them. My favorite is the magret or boned breast of the Moulard, a large duck bred from a Pekin female and a male Muscovy and raised for its fattened liver. Magret de Moulard can be found in high-quality markets or ordered directly from dartagnan.com, which sells magret as a by-product of its foie-gras business.

MAGRET DE MOULARD Each half-breast weighs about a pound and serves two. You will need a cast-iron or heavy steel skillet, and a very sharp knife to score the skin through the fat but not into the meat in the finest cross-hatch you can manage. Lay the breast skin side down in the hot skillet, and reduce the heat so as to render the fat slowly without overcooking the meat, which must be served pink and warm: no more than 125 degrees on an instant-read thermometer, or even less, according to taste. Above all, do not overcook the magret.

Pour off and save the fat as it accumulates: use it to braise a few turnips in three-quarter-inch dice. In about ten minutes, nearly all the duck fat will have been rendered. Then turn the breast over and sear the other side over high heat for a few minutes, until the meat feels firm to the touch. Keep the magret warm under a kitchen towel or in a barely warm oven.

Meanwhile, prepare Colonel Hawker's Sauce.

Colonel Hawker is said to have been Wellington's fowling officer in the Peninsula Campaign of 1809. My late dear friend, great editor, wise counselor, and fine cook, Angus Cameron, gave me this recipe years ago, and I have used it often for duck both tame and wild, venison, wild boar, and so on.

COLONEL HAWKER'S SAUCE

Chop three shallots coarsely, and sauté them in a tablespoon of duck fat or butter or a combination of the two. When the shallots have softened, add a tablespoon or so of arrowroot to make a roux, and cook for a minute or two. Add a cup of warm veal and duck demi-glace, which you can also order from D'Artagnan; a tablespoon each of Harvey Sauce and Mushroom Ketchup, nineteenth-century English condiments that you can order from the British Shoppe (1-800-842-6674) or thebritishshoppe.com (or substitute Worcestershire); juice of one lemon; four whole cloves; one teaspoon ground mace; and a half-teaspoon of cayenne. Reduce this slowly to about half its volume, then pour in a glass of good but not great port, and reduce again by half. Strain out the vegetables and spices, and boil down to thicken slightly if necessary. Cut the duck breast on the bias across the grain about a quarter-inch thick, or more or less as you like, fan it out nicely, and nap with the sauce. Serve with braised or sautéed turnip or puréed celeriac and a mélange of wild mushrooms.

SEVEN

AVE HOMARUS
AMERICANUS

The joys no less than the agonies of childhood
become the substructures of maturity. I remember
long summer excursions a lifetime ago with my cousins
to the lobster pound at Pemaquid Point, on the Maine
coast, where, in a pine grove on a headland above a
pounding sea, at tables of varnished pine, we ate lobster
from steaming kettles of seawater; preceded by buckets
of soft-shell steamer clams, which we dipped in mugs of
clam broth to wash away the sand and then in drawn butter, in which we also dipped our lobster chunks. In winter there were lunches at Locke-Ober in Boston with my
father, who referred familiarly to the grand old restaurant, with its dark paneling and gleaming silver, as Frank
Locke's, insider's lingo of the previous century, and
introduced me—I could have been no more than
twelve—to the great Washington Street merchants,
plump, red-faced, in their gray double-breasted suits,

sipping their scotch and sodas at the other tables. There, in this dining room for men only, our lobster Savannah was served under silver domes by immaculate Irish waiters with thinning white hair and long white aprons who spooned hash-brown potatoes in cream into side dishes. Then around the corner to Summer Street, where at Bailey's we stood amid the damp furs of Christmas shoppers at the marble counter where other pink-faced men in spotless white aprons topped conical scoops of rich vanilla ice cream in hammered-silver stemware with hot fudge, marshmallow, and pecans, so generously applied as to spill over into the saucer, a Bailey's tradition.

In a recipe that I contributed to the *New York Times Magazine* a few years ago, I described my surprise when I was preparing to grill a dozen or so lobsters, those companions of my childhood, in my Sag Harbor kitchen. This meant killing them first by plunging a stiff boning knife into the shell just behind the eyes, drawing the knife forward to split the head, and then reversing the blade to bisect the entire creature from head to tail. I had piled the lobsters on a counter next to the sink and, with no more consideration for their feelings than if I were opening an oyster or peeling a potato, reached for the first victim and split it in two. To my surprise, the other lobsters raised their claws in horror at what I had done and scuttled en masse backward. Some fell to the floor, others into the sink. I was faced with a dilemma, for it was plain that lobsters were not at all unfeeling like the potato, but kindred souls who dreaded violent death as much as you or I do.

I wish I could say that I snipped the rubber bands from the claws of the survivors, took them down to the bay, and let them go. Instead, I gathered them up and killed each one out of sight of the others. It was late. Guests were on their way, including my neighbor Craig Claiborne, the *New York Times* food writer, whom I had invited to try my new lobster recipe, and I had nothing else on hand except a shoulder of lamb, and no time to marinate and braise it. Moreover, to spare a lobster by eating a lamb was morally absurd. Though I offered this argument in my article, readers were offended and accused me of being as cold-blooded as the lobster itself. Nevertheless, my moral logic is correct—killing a lobster is no more brutal than eating a lamb killed by someone else. We are omnivorous: facing starvation, as our remote ancestors must have done much of the time, we will eat almost anything, including one another. In times of famine we still do. According to the anthropologist Marvin Harris, citing Cortés's diarist, Bernal Diaz, the protein-starved Aztecs fattened their captives in cages and delivered them to priests to be butchered. Atop a pyramid, the priest removed the living heart while his assistants threw the arms and legs to the bottom, where they were boiled and served with *moli* sauce. Cortés himself witnessed an Aztec man eating a cooked baby for breakfast. Harris, who, like Freud, believes that our strongest taboos reflect our greatest temptations—we do not taboo putting our hand in the fire—conjectures that we taboo cannibalism not from high-mindedness but lest we be eaten ourselves. My friend Patrick O'Connell, the great chef/proprietor of the Inn at Little Washington, agrees. When I suggested some years ago that cooking for others is a gratuitous act of generosity, he said no: we feed others so that they won't eat us.

There are other ways to cook a lobster besides cutting it open and grilling it, but, whatever method you choose, care must be taken not to toughen the meat by overcooking it, nor should it be undercooked. Some years ago, in Provincetown, where I was visiting my dear friends the late Norman Mailer and his splendid wife, Norris, we stopped at a lobster shack to pick up a couple of three-pound females. Norman had been a cook in the army and still liked to tinker in the kitchen, but on this occasion I was left alone to make our supper.

LOBSTER FRA DIAVOLO

I made a spicy marinara in a large porcelain cocotte by softening in olive oil some chopped onion, garlic, jalapeño, and celery, then adding a large can of San Marzano tomatoes together with some fresh midsummer tomatoes from the garden, a good handful of dried oregano, and a generous pinch of sea salt and fresh-ground black pepper, and left it to cook down with a little red-wine vinegar to taste. While the sauce was thickening, I cut the lobster tails laterally into two-inch sections, and in a separate pan seared the exposed meat in olive oil over a high flame until the aroma of the scorched shells filled the Mailers' seaside kitchen. I then twisted the claws from the bodies and boiled them for ten minutes or so, cracked them with the back of a heavy knife, and dropped them, along with the tail pieces, into the warm marinara. After a minute I turned off the stove, leaving the lobster to finish cooking in the marinara but taking care to serve the dish before the lobster sat too long in the sauce and became ropy and dry. You will know when the lobster is done if it slips nicely from the shell with a few pokes of a fork. If it's underdone, it will stick to the shell. If it's overdone, it will slip from the shell without your help. You may cut into a piece to make sure it's opaque, resilient, but tender all the way through. With a shower of fresh Italian parsley from the garden, chopped not too fine, and a sprinkling of hot pepper flakes to taste, this is what old-fashioned Italian restaurants call "fra diavolo."

We ate the lobster over linguine with a bottle of Chablis beneath a perfect sky on the Mailers' deck, facing the long curve of the town as it wraps itself around the bay.

SWORDFISH WITH MARINARA The same marinara with an extra half-jalapeño, chopped; some pitted black olives; a small handful of capers, rinsed; a glass of dry white wine; fresh-ground black pepper; enough sea salt to bring up the flavor; and a generous handful of chopped Italian parsley to sprinkle atop the finished dish does wonders for swordfish.

While the marinara is thickening, pat dry about eight ounces of very fresh swordfish per person, and in a hot steel pan filmed with a little olive oil brown the fish on both sides quickly, just enough to cook it through. Then serve the fish immediately, napped generously with the spicy marinara, sprinkled with the coarsely chopped flat-leaf parsley. Be careful not to overcook the fish, which should be tender but firm. If the swordfish is left to linger in the sauce too long, the fish will become dry and the sauce watery.

CHICKEN UNDER A BRICK

When I reminded Norris recently of this lunch, she remembered another time, when we bought some young chickens—pound-and-a-half pullets, as poussins or game hens were called then, and what my late friend Sal Iacono called teenagers—butterflied them by removing the spines, fitting the tips of the legs through slits in the skin, folding the wings back to expose the breast, and pounding the birds flat with the side of a cleaver. This made a considerable racket in Norris's spotless kitchen, which must have alarmed her, since she remembers the scene vividly while I had forgotten it. The idea was to cook these chickens lightly oiled in a dry pan under a brick or similar heavy weight, so that if all goes well the chickens will emerge from the process looking like lacquered road kill, a chicken pancake with the curve of the legs and thighs a mere tracery against the crisp skin of the flattened breasts. This is a famous Italian dish—pollo al mattone, or chicken under a brick—with an intense chicken flavor, since nothing is lost in the cooking, especially the chicken's own aromatic fat. Norris remembers that when I had placed the lightly oiled chickens in a hot steel pan and fitted two foil-wrapped bricks over them, so that the entire surface of the birds touched the pan to brown evenly, I said that I needed a nap and asked her to reduce the flame and turn the birds over every five minutes, so that they would cook through without burning on either side. This request, which I had also forgotten, must have alarmed her even more than my pounding the chicken, since she recalled the moment with a shudder. When I make this dish now, I use a veal pounder rather than a cleaver, and a heavy pot half full of water instead of a brick, a less dramatic but quieter technique. And I finish them in a 350-degree oven for four minutes rather than risk scorching them in the pan.

On hot summer afternoons, I like to serve lobster rolls like those I made for our houseguests when we were first able to leave Manhattan for Sag Harbor after 9/11. (See page 46.) I like the way Hellmann's mayonnaise supplies the true, slightly tangy, not too oily Maine-coast flavor, and the look of the warm rolls lightly browned in butter and overflowing with cool lobster salad, on their platter, surrounded by frilly homemade potato chips, as the sun filters through a Murano-glass pitcher of Pinot Grigio, casting a yellow glow on the pink tablecloth on our terrace table.

For a first course at lunch a one-and-a-half-pound lobster will serve two, and for a main course at dinner each guest should be served a whole one. Be sure that your fishmonger gives you hard-shell lobsters. I buy them from a wholesaler in Chinatown all year round. Lobsters whose shells are pliable or soft will have recently molted and not yet grown into their new shells, which will be full of water for which you will be paying lobster prices. Ask for females. The eggs, called coral, turn red when cooked and have an intense lobster flavor. Not everyone appreciates this intensity, but it adds greatly to lobster salads and bisques.

Whatever their size, the lobsters should be vigorously alive before they are split and placed under a broiler, or dropped headfirst into two or three inches of rapidly boiling salted water and steamed, for ten minutes for one-and-a-half-pounders and as much as twelve minutes for two-pounders. If you boil more than one at a time, add a few minutes. After some trial and error you will be able to judge for yourself how long it takes the meat to reach the right temperature. It is better to err on the side of too little rather than too much, since you can always return an underdone lobster to the pot or broiler, but one that's overdone can't be rescued. Some people claim that headfirst into the pot is less painful than tail-first for the lobster, but how can they know? Others suggest anesthetizing them in ice water for half an hour, but since ice water isn't much colder than the seawater in which they live, this doesn't seem a likely solution, and leaving them in the freezer is probably no more humane than simply killing them at once. Whichever way they enter the pot, they will thrash about for a few seconds, but this is said to be only a final shudder of their primitive nervous system rather than an attempt to escape. I'm not so sure.

The boiled or steamed lobster will of course have turned bright red. Set it right side up, run some cold water over it, and when it is cool enough to handle, tie a large napkin around your neck, twist the tail from the body, and with a heavy knife split both body and tail lengthwise in two; then lift the tail meat out with a fork. If the lobster has cooked long enough, the meat will lift out easily. With the back of a heavy knife, crack the claws and knuckles and, using a small fork or lobster pick, extract the meat. For appearances' sake, you might try to extract the claw meat intact by wiggling the small part of the claw until it breaks away and the meat slides out. Place the claw and knuckle meat in the body cavity along with the red coral (eggs) and the unctuous, green-ish liver called tomalley. The lobster may now be served, either warm with an optional splash of lemon juice and an obligatory dip in drawn butter, or lightly chilled, but not ice-cold, with homemade mayonnaise, in this case thinned with a bit of lemon juice mixed with snipped chives and fresh tarragon. If the lobster seems tough, fla-vorless, yet cloying, you will know that you have over-cooked it and will do better the next time. Likewise, if the meat sticks to the shell and seems watery, you will know that you have not cooked it enough.

The fashion in the 1950s in such dishes as lobster

thermidor or Newburgh was to remove the cooked meat from the shell and finish it in a flavored béchamel with sherry, mushrooms, mustard, cream, tomato paste, Pernod, Cognac, and so on, in various combinations, and return it to the shell or place it in a gratin dish, sprinkle it with crumbs and/or grated cheese, and finish under a broiler. These concoctions are seldom if ever seen today.

I discovered my favorite lobster dish a few years ago in a book called *Les Dimanches* by Joël Robuchon, the French genius endowed with the minimalist culinary instincts of a haiku master. It is an utterly simple preparation which magically intensifies without violating the lobster's unique essence. Robuchon prefers Brittany lobsters over the American variety, but this is mere chauvinism, for, except that the European lobster shell is blue and the American shell is greenish black, there is no discernible difference. Both turn red in the pot and taste the same. Equally fanciful is his tender description of lobster lovemaking when the female has molted but the male is still in his armor, and of the lobster's suicidal affection for the conger eel. There is nothing fanciful, however, about his poetic treatment of lobster in Sauternes.

ROBUCHON'S LOBSTER IN SAUTERNES For two as a main course at lunch, or for four as a first course at dinner, you should boil two pound-and-a-half lobsters in lightly salted water for three minutes, cool them under cold water, and remove and return to the pot the large claws and knuckles for three more minutes. Then remove and cool the claws under cold water, crack them open with the back of a heavy knife, and extract the meat as nearly intact as possible by wiggling the smaller of the two pincers until it breaks away. Discard the legs, and set the bodies and tails aside, along with the claw meat. In a heavy cocotte just large enough to hold the two lobster bodies and tails, melt a half-stick of butter and soften a handful of diced carrots. Then chop and add two or three shallots, and when they are soft, pour in three cups of good but not the most expensive Sauternes and a cup of orange juice, a thin slice of fresh ginger, julienned, and a good pinch of the best saffron, with just enough sea salt to bring the flavors together. Bring the mixture to a rapid boil, and poach the lobster bodies in the covered cocotte for three minutes. Turn off the flame, and let the cocotte sit, covered, for four minutes. When you lift the lid, the aroma will delight you. Remove the bodies, and save the upper part for bisque or discard. Warm the reserved claw meat in the Sauternes mixture without cooking it further, and remove the meat from the tails, saving the shells for bisque if you are so inclined. The meat should be rather firm but not tight. Cut it neatly into one-inch segments, and on a luncheon plate reconstruct the tail halves in their original curved configuration (in the shell, if you like) so as to surround the claw meat, and nap with the reduced and strained Sauternes sauce.

The best lobster bisque I have ever tasted comes from the Seafood Shop in Wainscott on Long Island. Their classic recipe yields thirty quarts and calls for ten pounds of lobster meat, four pounds of onions, two bunches of flat parsley, one pound of butter, one quart of sherry, a tablespoon each of white pepper and celery seed, the "guts"—i.e., the tomalley and coral from the cooked lobsters—eight quarts of water, one pound of lobster base (a commercial product, an intense reduction of lobster shells and vegetables), one pound of cornstarch, eight quarts of heavy cream, and three bunches of scallions. A quart of this rich bisque will serve four. Given the superiority and convenience of the Seafood Shop bisque, I no longer make my own, but when I did,

LOBSTER BISQUE I boiled a three- or four-pound lobster for fifteen or so minutes in just enough water to cover and a glassful of white wine, extracted the meat, cut it in one-inch pieces, and broke the shells into small pieces under a dish towel with a mallet. I melted a stick of butter in a four-quart kettle and sautéed a cup each of chopped carrots, onion, and celery until softened, then I added the lobster water, plus an additional quart of water, and chopped shells and simmered the mixture gently for an hour or so. Toward the end, I added the tomalley and coral, some dry sherry, a little white pepper, a dash of Tabasco, and salt to taste. Then I strained out the solids, including the shells, ground them in a food processor with a little of the liquid, and pressed the ground mixture through a strainer into the rest of the liquid, creating the equivalent of the Seafood Shop's commercial lobster base. I mixed a tablespoon of cornstarch or arrowroot into a cup of the liquid, returned it to the pot with a half-cup of heavy cream and a little lemon juice to taste, and stirred the mixture over a low flame until it thickened slightly; then I added the lobster meat, sprinkled some chopped green onion, some snipped tarragon and parsley on top, and adjusted the seasoning. This is not as complicated as it sounds, but if you factor in the cost of the ingredients and the time spent at the stove, the Seafood Shop bisque is the obvious choice. Perhaps someday the Seafood Shop will freeze its bisques and chowders and offer them online.

Eventually, the brilliance of Robuchon's lobster in Sauternes will fade with familiarity, and I will return to an old favorite, Jasper White's pan-roasted lobster, the very dish I was preparing when my lobsters raised their claws in horror and bolted. I discovered this dish in Jasper White's Boston restaurant and later found the recipe in Julia Child's *In Julia's Kitchen with Master Chefs.* It is practically foolproof, takes ten minutes from start to finish, and beautifully combines the tender lobster with olive oil, Cognac, shallots, chives, and tarragon, a heavenly combination. Turn the oven on to 500 degrees and

JASPER WHITE'S PAN-ROASTED LOBSTER

bring a two-quart pot of water to a boil. Split two pound-and-a-half hard-shell lobsters by placing them top side up on a cutting board and plunging a stiff boning knife into the head, just behind the eyes, splitting the head in two. Then turn the knife the other way and split the body and tail. There is no reason to be squeamish about this. The lobster will die immediately, though it may continue to twitch as its nervous system subsides. Remove the black vein from the tail, discard the eight small legs, twist off the claws, and separate the lobster halves so that you can manipulate them easily when you pan-roast them. Poach the claws in the boiling water for five minutes. Cool them under cold water, and crack them open with the back of a heavy knife. Remove the claw meat in one piece if possible, by wiggling the small part of the claw, and in large chunks from the knuckles. Heat two skillets, each large enough to hold one lobster, or a single skillet large enough for two. I use a twelve-inch nonreactive skillet, which just accommodates the four halves. When the skillets are hot, film them with good-quality olive oil. When the oil shimmers, add the lobsters, shell side down, and turn them with tongs this way and that, until the shells turn red all over. Add more oil if necessary, but keep the flame high. In three or four minutes, the shells will be red. Turn the lobsters over for a minute or so, long enough to sear the meat, and pop the pan or pans into the hot oven for three minutes. Remove the pan or pans from the oven with a damp towel. The handles will be fiercely hot. Put the lobster halves on a platter, shell side down. The shells may be slightly charred at the edges. Test for doneness by lifting the meat from the shell with a fork. If it lifts out easily, it's done. If not, return it to the oven for another minute or two. Then remove the lobsters to the platter. Add butter to the pan or pans, and sauté some chopped shallots until they soften. Pour three shot glasses of good but not great Cognac into the pan or pans, stand back, and flame the heated Cognac with a butane lighter or a long match, or simply heat the Cognac and tip the pan gently toward the flames until the vapors ignite. Don't be alarmed—the flames will quickly subside. Then combine the contents if you are using two pans. Add a glass of medium-dry white wine, the claw meat, and some chopped tarragon and snipped chives, and reduce slightly over a high flame. Then, with the burner off, stir in half a stick of cold butter, a chunk at a time, stirring as each chunk melts, until the sauce has thickened slightly. Stuff the claw meat into the chest cavities and ladle the emulsion over the lobster. Serve while hot with homemade potato chips or matchstick potatoes (see page 32). It sounds complicated, but after you've tried it a few times it will seem easy.

EIGHT

WHY THEY
ARE CALLED
CHOPSTICKS

Some years ago, when I lived the life of a family man in one of those two-story, skylighted ateliers in the genteel bohemia of West Sixty-seventh Street, I dreamed of living one day in the far-west, as yet ungentrified, industrial reaches of Greenwich Village, or on the shabby border of Chinatown, still contained in those years within a few blocks of Chatham Square. I imagined entering through a narrow, dark iron doorway, set in a nondescript façade behind which lay a hidden pleasure dome of Ottoman gardens and splashing fountains. There, under dappled light, I would cook for friends and family and even agreeable strangers, who would come and go as they pleased. I have no idea from what fragments of childhood memory this fantasy of a pleasure dome arose, but the persistence of these buried memories led me to my present address, not far from where SoHo and the touristic remnants of Little Italy converge at the encroaching northern boundary of rapidly expanding Chinatown.

SoHo is the stylish neighborhood south of Houston Street (hence SoHo) of million-dollar lofts carved out of antebellum grand emporiums with their cast-iron façades and bold fenestration. In the 1950s, this vital area was threatened with demolition by an insane scheme to build a multilane highway across lower Manhattan, from the Holland Tunnel to the Manhattan Bridge, which would obliterate the thriving neighborhoods between Houston and Canal, including the Italian and Chinese districts, while cutting the island in half at the waist. It was my friend and author the late Jane Jacobs, the savior of cities, who organized the neighborhood to protest this scheme and after a twelve-year struggle prevailed over the highwaymen, developers, and their servile politicians. The result is one of the liveliest, most architecturally distinguished and varied parts of the city: indeed, of any city.

Here, on a typical morning, I walk along Grand Street with my dog, Hamlet, who drags me willingly at the corner of Mott into Di Palo's sublime cheese shop, a Manhattan landmark and the most illustrious of the few remaining institutions of the old Italian neighborhood, its counters piled high with wheels of Reggiano, Montasio, and Piave, its polyglot customers chatting as they wait their turn. Then, when Hamlet has had his morning snack of pecorino, we dodge Chinese butchers' boys in long white coats with dressed pigs slung over their shoulders, and forklifts laden with winter melons and crates of bok choy, and cross Grand Street to enter the teeming Chinese market along both sides of Mott between Grand and Hester, the liveliest of several such markets in what has become a vital Chinese city tucked into the city of New York.

I am expecting a guest for lunch and am looking at sea bass displayed in an outdoor stall, atop a bed of crushed ice, their black scales glistening in the pale winter sun. The trawlers must have hit a good school, since all three Mott Street fish markets display these three-pounders in abundance. Prices, as usual, are mysteriously uncoordinated, reflecting the bargains struck earlier this morning at the wholesale market—$3.19, $3.24, $3.20—but will soon be coordinated as the penny-wise shoppers assert their power. At the stall where I usually shop, the bass are marked $3.20. I shop here not because the price is lower by a penny or the quality higher: quality here is policed by the finicky customers and seldom a problem. I shop here because the clerk and I are used to each other. I jabber at him in English, and he jabbers at me in Chinese, and somehow we understand each other. I select a plump bass, check its eyes for brightness and its gills for redness, and hand it over to be scaled and filleted. With a shout, which I assume means fillet, the clerk tosses my fish to a colleague at the rear of the stall to be scaled and boned. How do you say "sea bass" in Chinese? I ask. "Seebah," he shouts excitedly, then, pointing to tilapia, sole, sardines, octopus, fluke, yellowfish, squid, and whiting, he rattles off their names in Chinese, none of which I understand, but I am pleased to know "seebah" and will use it next time.

Beside me stands an ancient Chinese gentleman bent over a box of live turtles, which have attracted Hamlet's interest as well. Because the turtles violate the city's humanitarian ordinances, the box had been partly hidden behind a wooden barrel half filled with frogs, gazing pathetically skyward. "Soup. Soup," shouts the clerk, gaily pointing at the turtles. "Twelve dollah. Fourteen dollah." I think of buying the entire box and letting its occupants go—but how and where? Would the SPCA take them? Instead, feeling cowardly, brutal, hypocritical, helpless, I cross the street with Hamlet to see if pea shoots—called "tau mee-yu"—might still be in season. I need a pound for lunch.

Chinese shoppers, many of whom are recent emigrants from the Chinese countryside, are unused to refrigeration and want to buy their fish live. This is impossible with wild fish, but farm-raised fish like tilapia, catfish, carp, or freshwater striped-bass hybrids are delivered every morning to Mott Street from black plastic tanks the size of backyard swimming pools mounted on flatbed trucks. Some are displayed for sale in bubbling aquariums. Live eels, catfish, and carp are sold from smaller tanks, or simply left to flap their lives away on piles of ice while Chinese grandmothers indifferent to this drama poke through bushel baskets of writhing crabs. Though non-Chinese are increasingly in evidence at these markets, most shoppers here are Chinese women who scrutinize every long bean and snow pea before parting with their money. On the day I bought my sea bass, green onions were three bunches for a dollar at one stall and four bunches for a dollar at the next stall. That same day, at a Whole Foods Market, scallions of similar quality were a dollar a bunch. In Chinatown, fat asparagus were $1.50 a pound, spinach seventy-five cents for a large bunch, and a pound of shiitake mushrooms $3.60. I was amazed to find littleneck clams at $4.25 a dozen, oysters at $4.00 a dozen, and langouste at $5.00 a pound. Fresh Portuguese sardines and octopus were $1.99 a pound. Six dollars gets you a pound of barbecued spare ribs, and for ten dollars you can buy fifty shrimp dumplings ready for steaming.

But these prices don't tell the whole story. In the fancy Chinatown shops specializing in rare delicacies, birds' nests to make a mildly flavored gelatinous soup base go for $2,380 a pound, wild American ginseng for $1,880 a pound, dried abalone for $495 a pound, and first-quality shark fin a mere $328 a pound.

The restaurants in Chinatown range from quite good to pretty poor, but they are on average good enough that I seldom cook Chinese meals myself, as I did when I lived uptown. But I do use the ingredients for my own concoctions. On the day I bought the sea-bass fillets, I also picked up a half-pound of mung-bean sprouts, a plastic bag of fermented black beans, some fresh shiitakes, green onions, a red bell pepper, and a piece of ginger. I also bought a package of ready-cooked Hong Kong yellow noodles. When Hamlet and I got home that morning, a half hour before my guests were to arrive, I cut two "x"s through the skin of each fillet without

STIR-FRY OF SEA BASS

cutting into the meat, to keep the fillets from curling up, and dropped the pre-cooked Hong Kong noodles into warm water to loosen them, drained them, and flavored them with a teaspoon or so each of dark sesame oil and soy sauce. I then filmed and heated a sauté pan with a little peanut oil and dropped three handfuls of noodles into the pan, which I shaped and flattened to the thickness of smallish pancakes. When the bottoms began to brown over a low flame, I turned them over and browned the other side, and set the crunchy noodles on three luncheon plates. To the same pan I added more oil and warmed some garlic, to which I added the bell pepper in small dice, some green onion split in one-inch segments, two shiitake-mushroom caps, sliced, and a large tablespoonful of fermented black beans chopped fine. I added a tablespoon of soy sauce and another of oyster sauce to the mixture and stir-fried for a minute or two. Then I added a cup of chicken broth from a carton and finished my stir-fry with a teaspoon of potato starch dissolved in a little water, cooking until the sauce thickened just a bit. Had it thickened too much, I would have added a little more broth. In a separate pan I warmed two tablespoons or so of oil, and when the oil was hot but not smoking, placed the bass fillets skin side down, side by side, and reduced the flame by half. Then I weighted the fillets with a heavy pot half filled with water, so that they would color evenly and not curl. After a few minutes, I removed the pot and turned the fillets over to cook for another minute, until the flesh was just cooked through. I placed the fillets skin side up atop the noodles, and poured the black-bean mixture over, adding a garnish of cilantro leaves with stems. Meanwhile, I washed the pound of snow-pea leaves (tau mee-yu), sometimes called pea shoots, in cold water, trimmed the stems, and heated a scant tablespoon of oil—you don't want the leaves to be too oily—in a wok in which I had lightly browned a garlic clove in the oil. Then I added the wet leaves. After a brief sizzle as the water hit the hot oil, I turned the leaves with tongs until they softened and the water evaporated. I served these with a dash of soy sauce alongside the bass.

Years ago, when I lived uptown, where the neighborhood Chinese restaurants were terrible, I taught myself to cook Chinese from a book. The *batterie de cuisine* was not complicated: a well-seasoned steel wok, a shovel-like Chinese scoop and ladle, some chopsticks, a sharp cleaver, wire strainers of various sizes with bamboo handles, a stockpot, and a few basic condiments, all of which were easily found in Chinatown at the time but now are routinely stocked as well in the Asian section of most supermarkets: soy, oyster, dark-sesame, and hoisin sauces; black beans in jars; five-spice powder; dried shiitake mushrooms; tins of water chestnut and bamboo shoots; peanut oil; fresh ginger root; star anise; and, of course, cornstarch, chicken stock, and inexpensive dry sherry. Today the variety of sauces, aromatic dried fish, pickled vegetables, fresh water chestnuts, bitter melon, bamboo shoots, and lotus root, spices, condiments, and so on stocked in Chinese food stores can be bewildering, but the basics will support a substantial repertory of simple Chinese dishes.

The book from which I learned the basics of Chinese cooking was called *How to Cook and Eat in Chinese,* by Buwei Yang Chao. It had been published in 1945 and was out of print, but I had found an old copy and eventually republished it in a paperback edition, which sold well but is now also out of print, lost in the avalanche of Asian cookbooks that have been published since. As far as I have been able to discover, Mrs. Chao's book is the first successful attempt to publish in English authentic rather than Westernized Chinese techniques and recipes. It includes more than two hundred recipes, with an informative introduction to Chinese culinary culture that covers ingredients, techniques, politesse, terms, and tools. Mrs. Chao's recipes are accurate and easily mastered, and her commentary remains fresh and useful. With her help I created my own polyglot improvisations long before fusion became the fashion.

The author explains that the word for chopsticks— "k'uai-tzu"—means "something fast," as when a rude tourist orders the waiter to move "chop-chop"; "small meals between meals" are called "tien-hsien," or "dot hearts," literally something to touch (dot) the heart. These are now transliterated as "dim sum," though when they first became popular with New Yorkers, before the Second World War, they were called "tea lunch," because, as the author explains, the Chinese typically do not drink tea with their three regular meals, but only with their dot hearts between meals.

Nom Wah Tea Parlor, on the dog-leg bend of Doyers Street in Manhattan's Chinatown, was serving tea lunch long before Mrs. Chao's cookbook was published in 1945, but as far as I can tell hers was the first book to introduce dot hearts or dim-sum recipes to American readers. Several common terms were coined by her with the help of her husband, Yuen Ren Chao, a distinguished if whimsical professor of comparative linguistics at Berkeley. For example, the term *ch'ao* "with its aspiration, low rising tone and all cannot be accurately translated into English. Roughly speaking ch'ao may be defined as a big-fire-shallow-fat-continual-stirring-quick-frying-of-cut-up-material with wet seasoning. So we shall call it stir fry. . . ."

Mrs. Chao was a physician who had "never stirred an egg" until she attended the Tokyo Women's Medical School, where she found the Japanese food "so uneatable that I had to cook my own meals." She adds, in an author's note to the first edition of her book, that "by the time I became a doctor I also became something of a cook." Since she admits that she hardly knows English, it must have been her scholarly husband who chose, in his wife's name, the word "eatable," from the Old English "etan," he explains, rather than the more pretentious "edible," imported from the Latin *edibilis.* In fact, it is obvious from the text that the professor wrote the entire book in his wife's name, using her recipes. This also explains why he coined the pronoun "hse" for "he/she" to refer to himself and his wife together, given the lack of a third-person singular pronoun of common gender in English except for the word "one."

I met the Chaos only once, when they visited New York. Professor Chao was tall, handsome, lean, and slightly stooped, with thick gray hair combed straight back, a Chinese Rex Harrison. His glasses were in the Chinese scholarly style, jet-black circles resting at the tip of his nose, and he wore one of those indestructible gray cardigans favored by elderly Chinese gentlemen at the time. His manner was shy, grave, affable—he was a punster. His wife, much shorter and excitable, was a plump canary, hopping from twig to twig. I could not understand a word she chirped. Had it not been obvious that the whimsical professor had written the text, I would have wondered why the Chaos were still on good terms, since the author's note was brutally insulting to the husband and their daughter, Rulan.

"I am ashamed to have written this book," hse wrote. "First because I am a doctor and ought to be practicing instead of cooking. Secondly, because I didn't write this. I speak little English and write less. So I cooked my dishes in Chinese, my daughter Rulan put my Chinese into English and my husband finding the English dull, put much of it back into Chinese again. Thus when I call a dish Mushrooms Stir Shrimps, Rulan says that's not English and that it ought to be Shrimps Fried with Mushrooms. But Yuen Ren argues that if Mr. Smith can go to town in a movie, why can't mushrooms stir shrimp in a dish?" To which one might reply that Mr. Smith goes to Washington under his own power, whereas mushrooms, being passive, must be stirred by the cook.

"I don't know how many scoldings and answerings back and quarrels Rulan and I went through. . . . Now that we have not neglected to do the making up with each other . . . it is safe for me to claim that all the credit for the good points of the book is mine and all the blame for the bad points is Rulan's. Next I must blame my husband for all the negative contributions he has made toward the making of this book. In many places he has changed Rulan's good English into bad which he thinks Americans like better. His greatest contribution is even more negative. Whenever a dish is not quite right or when it is repeated too often he simply leaves it alone."

Pretending to be his wife, Professor Chao writes, "Making others feel at ease is as true of Chinese manners as of American manners, but we apply the principle very differently. Sometimes we seem to be actually quarreling and fighting when we are really each trying to be more polite than everybody else. The important thing is that in that wrangling atmosphere everybody feels happy and at ease, because things are going as they should."

Several of Mrs. Chao's basic recipes have inspired the more complicated versions in later Chinese cookbooks, and several of his/her attempts to create an equivalent vocabulary in English have become part of the culinary language, such as "stir-fry" and "pot stickers." Mr. Chao's attempt to introduce "ramblings" for "hunt'un" (wonton), "which differ from ordinary, neat-edged wraplings by having fluffy or rambling edges like the tails of a goldfish," didn't catch on. But Professor Chao adds this footnote: "The same spoken word, written differently, means in fact the nebulous state of confusion when the world began," an elevated thought to accompany your next bowl of hun-t'un soup.

How to Cook and Eat in Chinese is once again out of print. My copy is brittle with age. Much of it is out of date. Today leaf lard is hard to find, but ginger is everywhere, and bok choy and hoisin can be found in most supermarkets. But the recipes are still basic and true. Perhaps in the digital future a virtual copy of the Chaos' book will turn up. If so, cooks will still find the recipes useful. They will not daunt amateurs and will inspire experts.

The other day, I ordered an oyster omelette in a neighborhood Malaysian restaurant. The eggs were cooked quickly over high heat and therefore were tough, the oysters were too small and too few, and the seasoning was off, a hasty job by a careless cook. Years ago, the Chinese omelette called "egg foo yung" could be found on Chinese restaurant menus practically everywhere. In the 1960s, Jane Jacobs, my ten-year-old son, Jacob, and I were exploring northern Canada at the northern terminus of the rail line at Moose Factory, a remote settlement at the foot of James Bay, a southern extension of Hudson Bay. Moose Factory consisted of some bleak Inuit dwellings, a run-down motel, and two Chinese restaurants bearing identical signs—"Mets Chinois et Canadien"—and probably owned by descendants of the Chinese crews that built the railroads and prepared their native cuisine themselves. The egg foo yung that we were served was an adequate relic of New York's Chinatown in a sub-Arctic wilderness. Now the dish seldom appears on New York's Chinatown menus. But I still serve my version of Mrs. Chao's authentic Cantonese oyster omelette. It's quick, easy, and delicious. Chinese fish markets and upscale supermarkets carry jars of shucked West Coast oysters, which cost less and are easier to use than local oysters in the shell, but if you can't find bottled oysters, the fishmonger will shuck some for you if you can't shuck them yourself. **For two,**

EGG FOO YUNG **you will need about a half-dozen medium oysters, six eggs, a handful of bean sprouts, a celery stalk chopped fine, a few green onions in one-and-a-half-inch julienne strips, two tablespoons of oyster sauce, a pinch of sugar, a smaller pinch of salt, sesame oil, and some cornstarch. Quickly stir-fry the oysters in peanut oil in a ten-inch pan or wok until they puff. Drain and save the oyster liquid, and reserve the oysters in a separate bowl. Then lightly oil the pan again, and toss in the bean sprouts, chopped celery, green onions, sugar, salt, and oyster sauce. Stir-fry over high heat for a**

minute or so, and add to the reserved oysters. Clean the pan, warm it, and film it again with peanut oil, and pour in the eggs, lightly beaten. Reduce the flame. As the eggs begin to form a bottom, mix in the vegetables and oysters, and cook the mixture slowly over moderate heat, lifting the edges from time to time to let the uncooked eggs flow to the bottom of the pan. Now fold the eggs with the filling in half—back to front, and cook the underside until it just begins to brown. Turn the eggs over, and cook the other side to the same point. Don't worry if some of the mixture falls out. Slide the omelette onto a warm plate. Thicken the reserved oyster liquid a bit over a moderate flame with a half-teaspoon of cornstarch dissolved in a little water, add a dash of soy sauce and sesame oil, pour over the omelette, sprinkle a few sprigs of cilantro, and you will have made a classic egg foo yung for two or perhaps three. You will also wonder why so few Chinese menus feature this unctuous dish.

Mrs. Chao's Chinese-style sashimi makes a good starter for an egg-foo-yung lunch. If you have the basic ingredients on hand and a good fish market nearby, you can whip it up in minutes, but you will have to let the dish stand for ten minutes or so while the fish marinates.

CHINESE-STYLE SASHIMI

You will need a very sharp thin-bladed knife with which to cut a pound of very fresh wild salmon, tuna, or wild striped-bass fillet, or a mixture of all three, into very thin, very neat oblong slices, as in Japanese sashimi. Then mix a tablespoon or so of dry sherry with another of soy sauce, a few grains (no more) of sea salt, a little fresh-ground pepper, a green onion trimmed and chopped very fine, and a teaspoon of sesame oil. Let the fish steep in this marinade in the refrigerator for ten minutes or so, and serve with a few sprigs of fresh cilantro.

Recently, my old friend Eddie Schoenfeld cooked for me and a few friends at his home in Brooklyn. I have known Eddie since the seventies, when I was startled one day at lunch with a Random House colleague at Uncle Tai's, then the hottest upscale Chinese restaurant in New York, to find what appeared to be a bearded Chasid in a black suit, but without the usual hat, and with a nonregulation black bow tie, handing out menus. Eddie was not a Chasid. He had begun his odd career by arranging banquets for his friends at authentic Chinatown restaurants, and soon this became a business. One of these restaurants had made a great success by introducing spicy Szechuan cuisine to the United States, and its owner, David Keh, decided to try his luck uptown with Uncle Tai in the kitchen. He took Eddie with him. Eddie brought his clients along. The place was a huge success. And so we met.

Our friendship took root and blossomed. I suggested to Eddie that he and Uncle Tai write a cookbook. Uncle Tai's so-called Hunanese recipes had caught on with uptown diners, and some would become classics, ubiquitous today on Chinese menus. To illustrate this success, Eddie multiplied for me the number of Chinese restaurants in the United States by the presumed propor-

tion that include General Tso on their menus and calcu-
lates that Americans now spend over a billion dollars a
year on these sweet, gooey, high-margin chicken thighs.
Later, Eddie explained that these were not necessarily
Uncle Tai's recipes, nor were they Hunanese. Hunan is
an impoverished province, and its cooking is undistin-
guished. But the name was easier to pronounce than
"Szechuan," and so Uncle Tai's enterprising backer,
David Keh, launched Hunan haute cuisine for the
uptown trade. Moreover, some of the recipes were actually created by Mr. Peng, a reclusive genius from Taipei.
Uncle Tai, a master chef with an unpredictable temper,
adapted many of his dishes for Americans. When we
signed the contract for the Uncle Tai cookbook, neither
Eddie nor I knew this complex provenance. Nor did we
know that Uncle Tai's third son would be furious with
Eddie for revealing his father's recipes, which the son
considered family property. On a busy evening at Uncle
Tai's, as Eddie was serving a banquet to a table of twelve,
the number-three son, a waiter and a judo expert, flew
at Eddie, who landed unconscious for a few minutes on
the carpet. Eddie, a cool professional, eventually got up,
arranged his tie, walked out of the restaurant, and never
returned. Uncle Tai's cookbook, which would probably
have become a perennial best-seller, was never published, but became the basis for Eddie's collection of
thousands of Chinese recipes. Uncle Tai eventually left
New York and reopened in Dallas.

At dinner in Brooklyn, Eddie recalled these events

in his cheerful, dispassionate way but concluded with a sigh: that night, he said, "we had a line out the door." Eddie has since created several fine Chinese restaurants in New York, most recently the Chinatown Brasserie on Lafayette Street, one of the two or three top Chinese places in town at the moment. The dinner he served that night was effortless and sublime. The main dish was a simple steamed salmon fillet about a half-inch thick, served in bite-size pieces beneath a sauce that requires careful measurements until you've made it a few times. Once you understand how the complex flavors blend— the fermented black beans are dominant, but faintly, like an echo; the oyster sauce provides body and salty sweet- ness; the sherry adds a delicate nip—you will have no trouble reproducing Eddie's dish, which, including prep, shouldn't take more than ten minutes, assuming you have the ingredients and equipment at hand. Salmon and fer- mented black beans are of course a well-known combi- nation, but this subtle treatment gives the traditional preparation a nice bounce. Serve it with mildly flavored fried rice, or precooked Hong Kong noodles, mixed with enough sesame oil and soy sauce to add a mild flavor.

SALMON WITH FERMENTED BEANS

You will need a twelve-inch bamboo steamer with a tight-fitting lid, a fourteen-inch wok, and a ten-inch heat-proof platter, lightly oiled so that the fish won't stick. For the sauce, you will need a small bowl in which to mix a half-teaspoon each of minced garlic, minced fresh ginger, and sugar; a teaspoon each of regular (Kikkoman, e.g.) soy sauce and dark soy sauce, blended with mushrooms, which you will find in Chinese food shops; two teaspoons of oyster sauce, available in many supermarkets; a tablespoon each of finely chopped fermented black beans (sold in Chinese food stores) and dry sherry; and a dash of fresh-ground white pepper. A quarter-teaspoon of MSG is optional and unnecessary. To the mixture add a teaspoon of potato starch if you can find it in a local health-food store—or arrowroot, or as a last resort cornstarch—dissolved in two tablespoons of water. Then put three inches of water in the wok, fit the steamer to it—make sure that the bottom edge of the steamer sits in the water, or it will scorch—and bring the water to a boil. Center two half-inch fillets on the oiled plate, pour the sauce over them, and sprinkle a half-cup or so of green onions over that. Put the plate in the steamer, and cover it tightly with the bamboo top. Do not use a metal top or the condensed steam will fall back onto the fish and ruin it. After three or four minutes, the fish should be barely cooked through at its thickest part. Break the fish up with a chopstick, mix the fish bits with the sauce, and serve at once. This is a wonderful dish for four; quick, easy, inexpensive, and delightful.

FRIED RICE For fried rice, boil two cups of rice with two and a half cups of water: I use basmati, but any unflavored standard long-grain rice will do. Boil until the water disappears, then cover and set over a very low flame to steam for ten minutes or so, until all the water is absorbed and the rice is just beyond al dente. If you overcook it, don't despair. Turn it into gruel by adding a little water and cooking it further, adding soy sauce, chopped meat or fish, etc., and serve it as congee. Otherwise, let the rice cool and dry for an hour or two or overnight. Then, in a wok, heat a quarter-cup of vegetable oil, and when the oil is very hot but not smoking, add the rice and shove it around with a Chinese shovel-like scoop if you have one, or whatever else serves the purpose. After a minute or two, when the rice is well coated with oil, add soy sauce sparingly to taste. Then break an egg into the rice and mix it about until the rice is well warmed. Now you can add whatever suits you—bits of meat, chicken, fish, shrimp, vegetables, bean sprouts, leftovers—but not too much.

NINE

PUBLISHING BOOKS
WITH KNIFE AND FORK

In the 1950s, when I lived on the top floor of an old town house in Greenwich Village, I could still encounter on walks through my neighborhood relics of the old bohemia: the wood-frame house on Bedford Street where Edna Millay once lived; Patchen Place, the rickety mews where e. e. cummings rented a house and where Djuna Barnes still lived; the run-down tenement across town, on St. Mark's Place, where Lev Bronstein, who changed his name to Leon Trotsky, once kept a printing press, and where Wystan Auden and Chester Kallman now lived, amid piles of books and manuscripts, and where you had to check before you sat down that Chester, a good if messy cook, hadn't parked a pot of oxtail stew on your chair. On Hudson Street, Dylan Thomas was drinking himself to death at the White Horse, two blocks north of the modest house where Jane Jacobs wrote *The Death and Life of Great American*

Cities. Once or twice in the Fourth Street subway station, when I still worked at Doubleday and Co., I saw William Faulkner—slight, with grayish hair, dressed in chinos—clutching a manuscript folder on his way uptown to see his editor, Albert Erskine, at Random House. It did not occur to me—as I walked along these century-old streets under leafy sycamores with Barbara and her Harvard friends John Ashbery, Frank O'Hara, and Kenneth Koch, who would become the so-called New York School of Poets—that we were at the end of an expiring bohemia, which was even then becoming gentrified. That trickle would soon become a flood of restored town houses, smart restaurants, and expensive shops, all but obliterating the picturesque remnants of the 1920s culture.

From my flat on Tenth Street, I liked to walk a mile or so downtown to the old Washington Market, which was razed by 1973 to make way for the World Trade Center. There are still a few old-style public markets in New York's ethnic neighborhoods, where merchants hire stalls to display their meat, poultry, produce, and grocery items, and from May to October the green markets throughout the city are a blessing, but the Washington Market, beneath a vast skylit roof bounded by Fulton, Vesey, and Washington Streets, barely a mile north of the tip of Manhattan, was special, for it had been established before the Revolution on land donated by Trinity Church and still conveyed a sense of those times. Here you could feel immersed in New York's living past as you wandered from booth to booth, tended by merchants with plump red faces in long white coats and straw boaters beside shambles offering racks of feathered game, fine poultry, sides of beef, whole lambs and piglets, while other stalls featured crates of eggs, tubs of yellow butter, neatly piled eggplants and cabbages and oysters on ice, one of which poisoned me so that I could not look at another for a decade.

I remember, as in a dream, a long-lost restaurant on Cedar Street, a few blocks north of the market, which must have supplied the game birds featured on its menu, including the cold Scotch grouse that I ordered at a solitary lunch some fifty years ago. The bird was boned and stuffed with foie gras and accompanied by a sprightly juniper-infused game sauce, with a side of pommes soufflées on a linen napkin in a battered silver dish. But a few years later, when I happened to be downtown, the restaurant had vanished, leaving not a trace. Even now when I find myself on lower Broadway I think of it and wonder if that unforgettable restaurant, with its sawdust floors and worn wooden tabletops, may have been only a dream.

For underpaid young editors in those days, there were a dozen or so inexpensive French restaurants in Manhattan with blurred menus in light-blue ink run off on a ditto machine, offering céléri rémoulade, moules marinière, pâté maison, maquerau au vin blanc, escargots, blanquette de veau, coq au vin, boeuf bourguignon, entrecôte aux pommes soufflées or frites, and so on, of which the Fleur de Lis on the Upper West Side was typical. Here two could spend a long evening, with a carafe of wine, for under ten dollars. For grand occasions there was Chambord, on Third Avenue, with its trolley of hors d'oeuvres, its soufflés, and its chocolate truffles to take as you left. Here you could spend forty dollars for dinner for two with a decent claret. When Chambord disappeared to make way for what would become the Random House Building, Roger Chauveron, the owner, opened a place around the corner in his own name, which lasted a few years, until it, too, was displaced, by the new Citicorp Building. One by one, Manhattan's other high-style so-called Continental restaurants followed Chauveron into oblivion, including the very chic Colony. It was there one night that I witnessed an old woman in blue sneakers, who had been canvassing the other diners for Richard Nixon earlier in the evening, pass out and apparently die at her table. Whereupon four waiters swiftly appeared, each lifting a leg of her chair tilted slightly back so that she would not slide off, and carried her out of sight on this improvised palanquin, while the surviving patrons, having glanced at this memento mori, returned to their pheasants and quenelles de brochet. Eventually, even the great Le Pavillon, and finally its offspring, La Côte Basque, gave up, as a wave of culinary fads, led by *la nouvelle cuisine,* supplanted these monuments to Escoffier and Monsieur Point.

The business of book publishing is done mainly in

restaurants, at lunch and occasionally at dinner. Staff meetings are held, calls are made, and paperwork is shuffled in the office. Lunch and dinner reservations are made there, but the real work is performed with knife and fork. It was, for example, over lunch in 1925 at "21," then an elegant speakeasy on East Fifty-second Street in New York, and still a high-testosterone hang-out for burnished Wall Street ninjas, male and female, that Bennett Cerf, a young vice president at the firm of Liveright and Company, offered to buy from the brilliant but wildly improvident Horace Liveright the Modern Library, which provided the stability on which the company and its staff depended. Bennett had bought his vice presidency with an investment of twenty-five thousand dollars in the chaotic firm, and now, having learned the business, wanted his own company. Liveright was desperate to repay money he had borrowed from his father-in-law, whose daughter he wanted to divorce. The deal was made over lunch, and Random House was launched, with Bennett and his friend Donald Klopfer as partners and the Modern Library as its cash cow.

PINOCCHIO AT "21"

One evening in the 1980s at "21," a fellow Random House editor and I were awaiting Roy Cohn, a regular at that place, who was dying of AIDS and wanted to publish his memoirs while he still had time. Like so many others, I had dreaded and despised Cohn for his cruel red-baiting as Joe McCarthy's chief counsel. Later, when I got to know him, I found myself surprisingly at ease with him. Roy, I discovered, was born without a conscience, a Shakespearean birth defect that he shared with Edmund and Iago, for whose frailty S. T. Coleridge invented the exquisite term "motiveless malignity." Roy believed in nothing and had no concept of truth. His condition may explain but hardly excuses his atrocious behavior, or redeems the harm he did to his country and the countless people he had gratuitously hurt as McCarthy's chief counsel. I was fascinated by him as a moral grotesque like Faulkner's Flem Snopes, the fictional twin of Karl Rove. After a lifetime in the book business, I tend to see people as fictional characters, as Humpty Dumpty, Dr. Casaubon, Emma Bovary, Captain Ahab: a professional deformation. For me, Roy exemplified star-quality wickedness. It was Norman Mailer, Roy's Provincetown neighbor, who introduced me to him. I believe that Norman saw in Roy possibilities like those he had seen in Gary Gilmore, the heartless killer who with a slight moral adjustment might have been the promising young man next door rather than the murderer of *The Executioner's Song.* Norman did not pursue this opportunity with Roy, a neighbor and friend.

That Roy might write a valuable memoir was inconceivable. But with strong editorial help, perhaps something could be salvaged from the helter-skelter manuscript pages he had shown me. To reject out of hand his wish to write a book would have been irresponsible. Roy knew Joseph McCarthy and his sinister retinue as no one else did. Moreover, in person Roy was nothing like the dough-faced consigliere with the hooded eyes whispering into McCarthy's ear at the Committee's televised hearings. To my surprise, I had come to like him and hoped that with the help of an editor, Cohn might re-create his complex character as the narrator of his own life: a very long shot, but worth a try, and he was paying for dinner.

As we discussed the manuscript, Roy told me that he had been raised as a New Deal liberal Democrat by his father, a politically connected New York judge. In 1944, he campaigned for FDR on West Seventy-second Street, the beating heart of New York's liberal Upper West Side. He retained his Democratic Party affiliation throughout his life. His conversion to anti-Communism, he told me, came when, as a twenty-four-year-old assistant U.S. attorney, he joined the prosecution of the atomic spies Ethel and Julius Rosenberg and was won over by the fervent young FBI agents assigned to the trial. A few days later, when I asked Roy how seriously he took the threat of Communist subversion, he said offhandedly, as an actor might dismiss his screen self as just a job, "Communism never worried me. It was Joe's thing." To me Roy never displayed strong political feelings of any kind. But the story of his conversion to anti-Communism by the young agents to whom he was attracted seems plausible.

Thus he became a hero of the Republican right and used these connections to shape his career. Had the opportunity arisen, he could as easily have become a Stalinist.

Roy told me that U.S. Attorney Irving Saypol, the chief prosecutor of the Rosenberg case, was "an idiot" and that he himself was alone responsible for the major government strategy which led to the conviction and execution of the couple. This strategy included a secret arrangement which he claimed to have negotiated with Joe Rauh, a famous liberal lawyer, to spare his client, David Greenglass, a Los Alamos machinist, the electric chair. Greenglass agreed to testify—falsely, as he later admitted—that his sister, Ethel, typed her brother's stolen notes, which Julius then forwarded to the Russians. This clinched the case for the prosecution. There was much potentially important material of this sort in Cohn's chaotic pages, and I had hoped that we might salvage enough of it to make a book before Roy died. But Roy was obviously dying when we met at "21," where he ordered his favorite tuna salad, made especially for him but left untouched that evening.

Roy was interesting on Judge Irving Kaufman, who presided at the Rosenberg trial and was Roy's neighbor on Park Avenue. Every evening during the trial, according to Roy, the judge and he would discuss ex parte the day's events and plan tomorrow's courtroom strategy without the presence of the defendants' counsel. When it came time to sentence the Rosenbergs, the judge, Roy said, asked him whether he should spare Mrs. Rosenberg's life, as Pope Pius XII, Albert Einstein, and Pablo Picasso, among many others, had urged, but the judge was unsure and let it be known that he sat for hours in Temple Emmanuel on Fifth Avenue consulting his God on the matter. According to Roy, the closest Kaufman came to the fashionable temple was the phone booth outside, where he discussed Ethel Rosenberg's fate not with God but with Roy, on the other end of the line, in Boca Raton. It was Roy, by his own account, who settled the matter by reminding the judge that the Rosenbergs were found equally guilty, so Mrs. Rosenberg's gender should not be a factor, though Roy may have known at the time that Greenglass's testimony was fraudulent. According to Roy, the judge asked how this would play in the *Times,* whose support he coveted. Roy told him not to worry and Ethel Rosenberg was sentenced to death.

Roy then went on to become McCarthy's chief counsel, an assignment that Joseph P. Kennedy wanted for his son Bobby. The elder Kennedy had paid McCarthy not to campaign in Massachusetts for the Republican candidate when Jack was running for the Senate in 1952 and felt that Joe owed him and his son a favor. But George Sokolsky, Hearst's political columnist, wanted Roy for the job, perhaps to show that not all Jews were Communists. With support from Cardinal Spellman and J. Edgar Hoover, according to Roy, Sokolsky convinced McCarthy to choose Cohn. Bobby was furious. He should not have been. Had he become McCarthy's chief counsel, the Kennedy family would have been ruined politically. Roy, by preempting Bobby, made Jack's presidency possible.*

One morning, in the kitchen of Roy's unkempt town house, I was pondering a cup of coffee that had turned cold as I waited for Roy to come downstairs to work on the manuscript. A back staircase led directly from the bedrooms to the kitchen. Eventually, Roy emerged wearing a short robe that reached only halfway to his bare knees. "Roy," I asked, "in your memoir, how do you plan to deal with your homosexuality?" I had found no reference to his sex life in his manuscript, though his preference was well known. In fact, at that very moment his companion, to whom I had been introduced previously, came down from the bedroom, said hello, and left. "Your homosexuality?" I reminded Roy. Roy and I belonged to a generation that had not yet gotten used to the word "gay." "I'm not homosexual," he replied, without expression, his watery blue eyes unblinking.

---

*Sokolsky's further contribution to history was his effort to promote the idea that the Communist takeover of China was the fault of a left-wing Democratic conspiracy. Roy told me that Sokolsky served as the bag man for the China Lobby, distributing money from Chiang Kai-shek's backers to various congressmen and others to support the Nationalist government in exile and, with the slogan "Who Lost China?," imply that the Democrats had handed the country to Mao. When I asked Roy how he knew this, he said, "I saw the boxes after he died." "What boxes?" I asked. "The boxes of money," he replied, and explained that he had been the executor of Sokolsky's estate, and the boxes of money in George's closet were meant for the China Lobby's propaganda campaign.

The bland country-club menu at "21" had never appealed to me except, *faute de mieux,* for the "black and blue" hamburger—a half-pound of chopped sirloin blackened on the outside, cool on the inside, steak tartare enclosed in a burnt hamburger crust—served with limp string beans and the restaurant's own spicy ketchup, tomato paste mixed with mustard, cumin, and who knows what else. That evening I didn't touch my hamburger. Roy was dying before my eyes. He could hardly lift his fork.

It was now obvious that he would never finish his manuscript. A few days later, I heard that Nancy Reagan had sent him to Walter Reed for experimental treatment with AZT. I never saw him again.

As far as I can recall, Roy never visited me in either Manhattan or Sag Harbor, but we did meet once at a restaurant in East Hampton. The occasion was the birthday of an old aunt, which Roy celebrated each year by inviting his most illustrious friends—politicians, tabloid journalists, judges, and so on—to a luncheon in her honor. But this year Roy was in disgrace. He had been disbarred for cheating a client, and his sickness had been widely rumored. His entourage had abandoned him and he would soon die. I arrived at the restaurant to find a long table set along either side for forty or so guests, with balloons and red, white, and blue favors at each place. But except for Roy himself and the old woman crumpled in her seat at the head of the table, no one had shown up. I was the only guest.

The "black and blue" hamburger that I ordered that night at "21" and couldn't eat is no longer fashionable, having been preempted by Daniel Boulud's extravaganza. But it is easy to make at home, and far less expensive.

"BLACK AND BLUE" HAMBURGER For my version, you will need a piece of rib eye or fillet, which you may grind at home in a food processor a little at a time, being careful to retain a chunky texture. What you want to achieve is room-temperature steak tartare enclosed in a shell blackened at top and bottom. Mix a few grains of sea salt, some pepper, and a trace of cumin or celery salt with a dash of Worcestershire into the meat. Form the mixture into a ball, placing a sliver of ice in the center. You might also add some celery and/or onion, chopped very fine. Lightly flatten the ball, top and bottom, and lower it carefully onto a well-seasoned, very hot cast-iron skillet or griddle to which you have added a knob of unsalted butter. After a few minutes, turn the burger carefully so that it blackens evenly, top and bottom. Then finish it in a hot oven until the sides are no longer raw and the burger holds together. The ice will keep the inside cool.

Roy's favorite tuna salad may not have strained the resources of the "21" kitchen, but at the far more ambitious Le Cirque, where Roy was also a favorite customer, a can of tuna must have been kept on its elegant shelf awaiting him, or perhaps the chef ruined a fine piece of fresh tuna by dicing and poaching it, mixing it with mayonnaise, some celery, and onion, and running it for a few seconds through the food processor. I never cooked for Roy, but had I done so I would have opened a ten-ounce jar of Italian tuna, processed it quickly with a spoonful of mayonnaise, some onion, celery, and sherry vinegar and served it with a few capers and a trimmed romaine heart dressed in black pepper and olive oil.

JACKIE O AT LUTÈCE

When I joined Random House in 1958, the offices were in the old Villard Mansion, the last such nineteenth-century palace left standing on Madison Avenue, in midtown, and now part of the Palace Hotel. My office was a former bedroom on the second floor with a balcony overlooking the courtyard. The place was charming, with creaking parquet floors and worn carpets, where authors might drop in for a chat unannounced or end a drunken night on one's office couch. At first there was more than enough space for our small staff. But as the book business expanded and came to rely increasingly on best-sellers, rather than publishers' accumulated backlists, requiring firms to risk ever more capital to acquire the rights to potentially popular properties, the smaller firms had no choice but to merge with the larger ones. Random House, having acquired Pantheon and then Knopf, had outgrown its old building, and moved with its acquisitions into a glass box on Third Avenue at Fiftieth Street, a few steps west of Lutèce,

New York's perennially best-in-class French restaurant until its great chef, André Soltner, retired in 1994.

André was from Alsace, and his superb cuisine, service, and ambience reflected his origins. The décor was appropriately luxe but understated for a three-star restaurant: the long garden room, under its barrel-vaulted glass ceiling with its banks of flowers, was spring-like throughout the year. The formal rooms on the second floor were in the correct Parisian high style. But the cuisine—celestial home cooking—owed more to André's Alsatian childhood than to Paris. Lutèce was, of course, expensive, and I dined there at Random's expense only on the most important occasions. One such time was the publication day of Elaine Pagels's now classic *Gnostic Gospels,* still in print after thirty years. To celebrate, I ordered a Corton-Charlemagne, shipped by Louis Latour. I forget the year, but the wine was an unforgettable Chardonnay, like one's first La Tâche of a great year, or the great Conte de Vogüé Bonnes-Mares of 1970 that I drank one night at the Connaught in London. What I noticed first was Elaine's look of shocked surprise. Then I tasted the wine and understood what had happened. Wine experts use the word "complex," but the actual experience was a melody, a fleeting musical phrase that rose and fell and rose again and slowly drifted away.

One day Jackie Onassis called me to ask if she could take me to lunch at Lutèce. We met a week or so later, on a fine early-spring day. My friend Pete Hamill, who had once taken Jackie out, said it was like "taking King

Kong to the beach." Jackie was one of those personages whom you do not accompany to a museum lest the visitors forget to look at the pictures. She didn't flaunt her celebrity but accepted it in good humor as the price to pay for being herself. We took a table upstairs, in one of the small rooms, and ordered shad roe, the first of the season. She asked if there was a job for her at Random House. She wanted to be an editor. She was obviously serious, and would attract interesting authors to the house. She knew everybody, read widely, and had excellent taste. I also knew that she could pick up within a few weeks the rudiments of the job. The rest takes a lifetime, but the rudiments would get her started. However, there was a problem. Entry-level editorial jobs were scarce and much in demand. The young assistants at Random, some of whom were excellent editorial prospects, had been waiting for such an opening for months—in some cases years—and were in the meantime performing routine tasks, hoping to be chosen. I told Jackie that I believed she would take the job seriously, be a good colleague, and learn the ropes easily. But I also told her that we would have to create an opening for her, and this might not be fair to the assistants. Before I could ask her to let me talk it over with my colleagues, she said that she understood my problem and didn't want to impose. I was grateful for her tactfulness but regretted the outcome. Eventually, she took a job at Doubleday, where she signed a number of interesting authors and worked until her final illness. I have wished ever since that she could have joined us at Random House.

Like everything else at Lutèce, André's shad roe was superb and easy to prepare, provided you treated it with care. Shad are available only in early spring as they move up the East Coast to spawn.

SHAD ROE WITH SORREL SAUCE

The roe are rather rich, and a single pair (the roe come in two banana-shaped lobes connected by a thin membrane) per serving are quite enough. If the roe are large, a single lobe is plenty. André prepared a sorrel sauce, the classic accompaniment. Sorrel first appears in the garden in early spring, when the shad are running. First wash a pound of sorrel and cut it in julienne strips. Warm it in a pot with some butter, and when the water from the sorrel has evaporated, add a pinch of sugar and a half-cup of heavy cream. When the sauce thickens a bit, take it off the stove. Then, with a very sharp knife, delicately separate the two lobes of the roe, being careful not to penetrate the egg sac. This will make it easier to turn the lobes as you brown them gently in butter. André dipped the roe in milk and dusted it in flour before adding it to the pan. I omit this step, but in either case sauté the roe over a medium flame—too much heat will generate steam and burst the sac—until lightly browned. Then, with a spatula in one hand and a wooden spoon in the other, carefully turn the lobe over and brown the other side, about three to six minutes per side, depending upon size. Do not overcook! The roe should be a little pink at the center. Set the roe on a platter and nap it with the sauce. Serve it with a lemon wedge, a few boiled and buttered potatoes, and a good Alsatian wine.

ADVENTURES WITH ALICE
AND OTHER GREAT COOKS

Inevitably, my interest in cooking led me to publish cookbooks, mostly by master chefs and bakers whose techniques I was eager to learn. These books sold well year after year, and some, like Alice Waters's *Chez Panisse Menu Cookbook,* became widely influential classics. A few professional chefs know how to adapt their recipes to domestic kitchens, which are unlikely to have on hand a gallon of veal stock, and even less likely to have reduced it to two cups of glace. But most chefs depend upon skilled cookbook writers to adapt and test their dishes, and these books usually lack personality. Not Alice Waters, however, whose vivid *Chez Panisse Menu Cookbook* was the first of many books by great chefs that I published. Alice was as meticulous an author as she was a chef, and a joy—if a demanding joy—to work with. With Alice, everything had to be just so: the jacket design, the typography, the binding, to say nothing of the writing itself. If she hadn't become a chef, she might have become a fine book designer, another craft in which style, precision, and taste are essential.

I did not seek Alice out. In the early eighties, she was a celebrity in the Bay Area, but her renown had not yet reached the East Coast. I met her by accident, and reluctantly. In the spring of 1979, I was in San Francisco and had made a dinner date with my friend Bob Scheer, a writer at the time for the *Los Angeles Times,* who had run unsuccessfully for Congress the year before. Alice had been Bob's campaign manager, and he suggested we go to her restaurant in Berkeley for dinner. "You'll like it," he said. I resisted. I still thought of Berkeley as a scruffy academic town of hippies, Hare Krishnas, and macrobiotic cafés. I wanted a nonideological dinner in San Francisco. Bob insisted. I submitted. We crossed the bay to Chez Panisse. I knew from the moment I sat down that I was about to be dazzled.

For dinner I ordered bouillabaisse, which turned out to be a silken fugue of textures and tastes whose clarity and honesty were poetry in a pot. I remember mumbling something to Bob that if Emily Dickinson owned a restaurant it would be Chez Panisse. Bob introduced me to Alice. I had not offered to publish a cookbook since the Uncle Tai mess, but I was besotted, and when Alice joined us at our table I proposed a contract then and there. I knew the book would become a classic. Moreover, I wanted her bouillabaisse recipe and hoped she would include it. She did: See page 176 of *Chez Panisse Menu Cookbook,* if you have a copy. This wonderful recipe appears in a section called "Uncomplicated Menus," an optimistic placement.

Her bouillabaisse for eight to ten fills three pages,

beginning with a marinade, then a rather complicated fumet, which becomes an even more splendid broth and a brilliant rouille. First she fillets and marinates eight

ALICE'S BOUILLABAISSE

pounds of firm, white, nonoily fish—halibut, striped bass, sea bass, snapper, etc.—in pieces of various lengths about an inch thick, in a half-cup of extra-virgin olive oil, two cups of dry white wine, two sprigs each of aromatic thyme and fennel tops, six parsley sprigs, three peeled garlic cloves, two tablespoons of Pernod, and a pinch of saffron, for an hour or so. She places in a separate bowl three and a half dozen littleneck clams and a dozen and a half Prince Edward Island mussels.

For the fumet, she cleans the fish bones, leaving no blood or gills (my fish market sells the fillets already boned, but supplies the bones and heads on demand), coarsely chops two carrots, a leek, a medium onion, two tomatoes, six mushrooms, and two garlic cloves, and cooks them with the bones in olive oil for ten minutes in a twelve-quart stockpot. Then she adds a bouquet garni of parsley sprigs, fennel seed, bay leaf, dried tarragon and thyme, a dozen peppercorns, and six coriander seeds; two cups of dry white wine; six mussels; six clams; the peel of a small orange (the pith removed); two tablespoons of Pernod; and a pinch each of saffron and cayenne. She simmers this for thirty minutes, skimming it often, lets it stand off the heat for fifteen minutes, and strains it, discarding the vegetables, shells, and bones. Meanwhile, she makes the rouille. She blackens a red bell pepper over an open flame and peels it, roasts and seeds a ripe tomato, and softens a slice of good Italian bread, crusts removed, in a quarter-cup of fumet with a pinch each of saffron and cayenne. She then beats three egg yolks into this mixture and slowly adds a cup and a half of olive oil to make a mayonnaise. She makes a purée of the peppers and tomato in a mortar and adds it to the rouille, which she adjusts with salt, pepper, cayenne, and saffron to taste. While this is happening, she rubs two dozen thin slices of baguette with garlic and oil and browns them in a 400-degree oven.

Then she makes the broth. In a quarter-cup of olive oil she sautés the white parts of two leeks, diced, and two medium onions, diced, with a large very ripe tomato, seeded and peeled, and adds a bay leaf, a pinch of saffron, the rest of the fumet, three cloves of garlic, minced, a sprig each of fennel and parsley, the peel without pith of half an orange, a cup each of white wine and Pernod, a pinch of saffron, and salt and pepper to taste. She brings this to a simmer, adds the mussels and clams till they open, and then the fish for a total of four minutes, or just until the fish are tender. Now she adjusts the seasoning as necessary with Pernod, cayenne, saffron, and so on. She serves the broth with the fish and shellfish in wide bowls garnished with the rouille and crouton. If you have the ingredients at hand, this is not nearly as complicated as it sounds. I usually shop in the morning for the fish and whatever else I don't already have, and put the dish together one step at a time throughout the afternoon, with long intervals of reading, gardening, or doing nothing.

Alice came to the table—a glowing half-pint, as she seemed in those days, with a huge smile—but I also sensed a wariness: the principled Berkeley purist, aglow with organic purity, girding herself against the corporate publisher from New York. Over soufflés and coffee, we agreed on terms that I wrote out on a scrap of paper. When I asked Bob Scheer about this recently, he said I might have used a paper napkin, but paper napkins were not Alice's style. Two years later, we published *Chez Panisse Menu Cookbook,* its handsome design supervised by Alice as meticulously as she plated her entrées. Her professionalism made her a joy to work with. With this book and those that followed, Alice redefined American culinary culture, French-inspired but based on fine local ingredients from artisanal producers with straightforward preparation and fine presentation.

We became and remain friends. On a summer weekend a few years later, she visited me in Sag Harbor, carrying a large transparent plastic box neatly filled with rows of peeled red, yellow, and green bell peppers in oil. She had been invited to Craig Claiborne's grand summer lunch party, to which each guest was asked to bring a dish. Since she could not safely have checked the peppers through to New York from San Francisco, she must have carried them on her lap all the way east, an indelible image of Alice in my mental scrapbook.

Craig Claiborne, the late food editor and restaurant critic of *The New York Times,* lived in East Hampton in a house that consisted almost entirely of a single large room with a restaurant kitchen at one end that opened onto a vast dining area—in effect, a private restaurant. Craig's bedroom was a cubicle behind a flush door at the far end of the dining room, and there were similar cubicles in the basement for his overnight guests. Craig liked to entertain, and twice a year he invited his favorite chefs, food writers, and friends to his house for large parties. His house was deep in a scrub-pine forest, and on New Year's Eve, his guests in formal clothes, and the chefs in toques bearing pots of cassoulet from their New York restaurants, made their way through the snow to be greeted by Craig in his blue-and-white-striped apron offering Dom Pérignon and Krug at the kitchen door. The deeper the snow and the colder the night, the more cheery the party became as Craig's guests settled gradually into a champagne buzz over their caviar, cassoulet, roast goose, and soufflés. By midnight, most of us were too far gone to drive home, but somehow we managed. I checked the *East Hampton Star* later that week to see which of us had landed in jail the next morning, but no one had.

Alice's invitation to Craig's annual summer party meant that she had been accepted into his pantheon. On the day she arrived, we had lunch in my garden: Gardiner's Bay oysters on the half-shell, and lobster rolls with curly potato chips, in dappled sunlight under my frail old cherry tree. This was her first experience of a Maine lobster roll, and she was suitably impressed. The following day, we drove over to Craig's, and soon I lost track of Alice in the crowd. Finding an unoccupied space on a couch, I asked the handsome woman with snow-white hair who had already taken refuge there whether I could join her. She was Maida Heatter, whose dessert cookbooks I had collected and treasured. I have forgotten what we talked about, but when I got up from the couch to find Alice and drive back to Sag Harbor, I had become Maida's publisher, and she invited me to her home in Miami for Thanksgiving.

Thanksgiving had always been my favorite or least unfavorite holiday, since, unlike Halloween, Christmas, and Easter, its pagan soul had not been turned into a marketing opportunity by monotheists. On eastern Long Island—amid the late-fall harvest, with rows of pumpkin, cabbage, and cauliflower still on the ground, and the cornstalks not yet cut—the ritual feast seemed real: a brined wild turkey stuffed with local oysters and corn bread and served with sweet local rutabaga mashed in butter. Because Lincoln had made it a national holiday, Thanksgiving also retains an element of the sacred, especially in Sag Harbor, with its Civil War monument and old houses, most of which, like mine, were standing just where they are today when that war was fought.

Maida's Miami, with its sea-washed sunlight, was not a typical Thanksgiving venue, but in her sunny kitchen, with its polished copper and its graduated nest of red Le Creuset pots, and her ginger biscotti, panforte, and chocolate brownies on the spotless counter arrayed as if for a photo shoot, everything was clean, well lit, and in its place, comforting, reassuring, mellow, with the Inter-coastal Waterway sparkling just beyond the glass doors to the deck. Maida's husband, Ralph, was alive then, and the other guests besides myself were Maida's great friend Wolfgang Puck, whose cookbooks I had begun to pub-lish; his wife, Barbara; and Craig. Judy, who was not yet my wife, had flown in from North Africa via Paris, arriving with a branch of fresh dates and a vacherin cheese just as Maida was lifting her magnificent popovers from the oven. Wolf had brought with him from Cali-fornia pumpkin soup and the turkey, which was now out of the oven. I brought caviar, Craig brought champagne; and so we celebrated the harvest.

My publishing career has been an extension of my for-mal education, a lifetime enrollment in a personal univer-sity whose faculty is the authors I publish and whose curriculum is their books. But with cookbooks the rewards can be more than merely intellectual. A dozen years ago, for example, I signed a contract with Frankie Pellegrino, the co-owner of Rao's, a tiny Italian restaurant with a mere ten tables on the corner of Pleasant Avenue and 117th Street in East Harlem, a relic of the old Italian neighborhood that had once flourished there, before East Harlem became Latino. Rao's is an intense distillation of that old Italian culture, and its tables are the de facto prop-erty of their longtime occupants: so-and-so "owns" table number one on Mondays, someone else has it on Thurs-days, and so on. So, to book a table when one of the regu-lars stays home, you have to call Frankie on his private number. I offered Frankie a contract for *Rao's Cookbook* not only because Rao's serves the best Southern Italian menu in New York, if not the world, and I wanted the recipes, but because I hoped that Frankie would award me a table of my own. My scheme backfired. *Rao's Cookbook* became a best-seller, and the demand for tables swamped Frankie's facilities.

One of the charms of Rao's had been that when you booked a table you had it for the night. You could sit over a bottle of wine and dessert and listen to the juke-box while now and then Frankie or one of his operatic customers would sing arias and others would join in. I was always surprised by the number of passable tenors at Rao's. But now that the book had become a best-seller, Frankie had no choice but to book two seatings and let people wait three deep at the bar for the regulars to leave. Before I published Frankie's book, I managed to eat at Rao's three or four times a year. Now I don't go at all. Instead, I make Rao's seafood salad, his orecchiette with broccoli rabe and sausage, and his chicken scarpariello at home. The dishes are utterly simple to prepare, and after the usual trial and error you will think they came straight from Rao's kitchen.

RAO'S CHICKEN SCARPARIELLO

For my slightly modified version of Rao's chicken scarpariello for six, you will need two three-and-a-half-pound chickens, spines removed, cut into eight pieces each, each half-breast with the first wing joint attached and the ribs removed, legs and thighs separated. Wash and thoroughly dry the chicken pieces, preferably overnight in the refrigerator, or with a hair dryer. Heat a half-cup of extra-virgin olive oil in a heavy pan or cocotte, and brown the chicken over medium-high heat, but don't cook it through. Remove the chicken, and drain it on paper towels. Cut two hot and two sweet Italian sausages into bite-size pieces, and brown these in the same oil. Remove them with a slotted spoon, and pile them up with the chicken. Then julienne two large bell peppers and a jalapeño (no seeds); halve and slice thin a medium-size sweet onion, and mince a teaspoon of garlic. Toss the vegetables in the oil, and cook them until they soften, adding more oil if needed. Remove the vegetables, drain the oil from the pan, and wipe it dry, then return the chicken, sausage, and softened vegetables to the pan. Add two hot, vinegared cherry peppers, a half-cup of red-wine vinegar, a half-cup of chicken stock, and a half-cup of dry white wine with a tablespoon of dried oregano. Cut three or four fingerling potatoes in half lengthwise, and put them in the pot. Cover the pot and cook gently until the chicken is just cooked through, five or six minutes. Do not overcook the chicken. Remove the chicken, sausage, and vegetables, except the potatoes, and reduce the sauce until it is slightly thickened and the potatoes are tender. Add salt and fresh-ground pepper to taste, and ladle the sauce over the chicken, sausage, and vegetables. The prep will take half an hour or so, but the dish itself could hardly be easier. Be sure to wash your hands after handling the jalapeños. You should be aware of but not overwhelmed by the heat from the jalapeños and cherry peppers.

RAO'S ORECCHIETTE

Rao's orecchiette (little ears) pasta with broccoli rabe and sausage is as easy to make as its name suggests. Set a pot of salted water to boil. Cut two sweet and two hot Italian sausages into one-inch pieces, and brown them, along with a garlic clove, in a heavy pot filmed with olive oil, large enough to hold a pound of cooked orecchiette. When the water boils, add a bunch of broccoli rabe with the ends trimmed to about an inch, and as soon as the water begins to boil again, remove the rabe with tongs and plunge it into cold water. Then drain, squeezing out as much water as possible, and coarsely chop it. Toss it in with the sausage, and reheat it. Then add a pound of orecchiette to the boiling broccoli water, and when it is al dente, lift it out with a Chinese strainer and add it to the sausage and broccoli rabe. If you don't plan to serve this at once, save the pasta water and use it to refresh the dish. Serve it with fresh-grated pecorino. It will be just as good as Rao's, but not nearly as much fun as eating it at one of Rao's tables in the old days, when Frankie would turn off the jukebox and a guy in the back of the room would get up to sing "Un Bel Di."

TWO COUNTRY INNS

For several years in the 1980s, when I was Gore Vidal's publisher and friend, we would meet in Paris, usually in the spring, and head south to tour the great restaurants of the provinces: Pyramide in Vienne, Pic in Valence, Troisgros in Roanne, Père Bis in Talloires on Lake

Annecy, Moulin de Mougins, L'Oasis, and La Réserve on the Riviera, to mention only those that come first to mind after so many years. These were splendid trips. Gore was a fine companion—learned, stoic, easy, generous, incapable of low thoughts or motives, but with a cool wit and a sharp tongue. He was then at the height of his powers. I shared his pleasure. He had a gift for friendship but harbored no illusions about human nature. He had come of age in FDR's Washington, amid the great nobles of the New Deal, and though he noticed the frailties of his distinguished elders, he regretted the long imperial decline from their Augustan moment.

Since neither of us was good at driving, especially after lunch—I think that Gore didn't drive at all—we hired a car and driver. We were told that he knew the local roads. One late afternoon, as we were heading south, the driver lost his way. I remember a road sign pointing to Mont-de-Marsan, but where this was in relation to our destination neither we nor the driver had any idea. It had begun to rain, and through the windshield I could see our forlorn driver at the roadside, holding a map, staring up at the Mont-de-Marsan sign, as helpless as ourselves. Gore meanwhile had opened his red *Michelin* and taken command. "We shall dine and spend the night at Magescq," he announced in his Napoleonic mode. "The route from here is direct." "What is Magescq?" I asked. "It is a two-star inn, in Les Landes. If we head into the sunset, we shall be there for dinner," Gore intoned as I scribbled a few notes. We retrieved our driver and were on our way.

Except for its church, its mansard steeple an inverted pot painted black topped by a spire, like the Kaiser's helmet, and the two-star Relais de la Poste with its pebbled courtyard, Magescq is little more than a widening of the old Napoleonic road from Bordeaux to the Spanish border. In a roadside field in the early-spring drizzle, the kitchen boys in their whites were kicking a soccer ball. Ours was the only car in the pebbled courtyard. The season had not yet begun. We were led upstairs to our rooms by the proprietor's daughter, a pretty girl in her early teens, her smile conveying the correct solicitude and distance, as if she had been performing these duties for decades. In the morning, she would appear in her robe to serve orange juice, croissants, and filtre in a breakfast room off the lobby. In my narrow room, where the bed occupied nearly the entire space, a card was propped against the phone with the number of the local doctor.

The dining room that evening was empty except for our driver at a corner table near the kitchen and a skeletal man and woman in matching black turtlenecks, who must have arrived after we did. They were silently sharing a *plateau* of Belon oysters. At the entrance to the two-star dining room, soigné but simple beneath an ancient beamed ceiling, were a silver tray of thrush and grouse in their feathers, and above them, propped against the wall, a larger tray of feathered woodcock, their beaks crossed like swords at a military wedding. These and a display of pheasant were framed by boxes of white asparagus, and baskets of morels, mâche, and fraises des bois.

That evening remains forever vivid in memory: the dining room with its soft lighting and aura of well-being; the hint of butter, shallots, and herbs in the air; the captain serving foie gras with green grapes from a porcelain cocotte, then pouring a perfectly chilled Sauternes; later, the salmon, so fresh that its eyes seemed to blink when it was brought to the table, and the white asparagus with its subtle hollandaise, and the Corton, and then the lamb. After a pause, some local cheese, a soufflé, filtre, Armagnac, in dated pots. Gore went up to his room with a bottle of Dom Pérignon. I lingered over coffee and Armagnac in the empty dining room until the lights were dimmed.

I have tried to duplicate this meal, as fugitive as a dream, with no success, but when I return to Magescq, it is as if I had never left.

The Inn at Little Washington, about an hour and a half south of the District of Columbia, with its whimsical elegance, glorious service, and superb kitchen, is my other favorite country inn, which, like Magescq, exists in a timeless world of its own, despite the sleek Washington notables who punctuate its dining room. I had been hearing about the Inn for years and meant one day to go there, but the trip from New York by plane to Dulles Airport and then by car to Little Washington seemed impossibly difficult. Then I came upon a remark by Patricia Wells, the Paris food critic, that her three favorite restaurants in America that year were Chez Panisse, the wonderful Café Boulud in New York, and the Inn at Little Washington. Since I had by then published the *Chez Panisse Menu Cookbook* and the incomparable Daniel Boulud's *Cooking with Daniel Boulud,* I picked up the phone and asked Patrick O'Connell, the chef/proprietor of the Inn, if he would like to make a third. So we met at the Inn, and the fine book that resulted is like Patrick, wise, elegant, honest, the result of years of discriminating practice, and, as he writes in the preface, "uniquely American though full of influences from other countries." *The Inn at Little Washington Cookbook* stayed on the *Washington Post* best-seller list for weeks. His lobster omelette with rainbow salsa is as easy to make as it is a joy to serve. It was awarded *GQ*'s Golden Dish Award as one of the ten best restaurant dishes in the world. How *GQ* managed to test all the restaurant dishes in the world to determine its list of ten is unclear. Patrick's lobster omelette is the school-lunchroom Spanish omelette with great panache, fit for a king's late supper with his lover or lunch with his wife the next day. For those who cannot make the journey to Little Washington, at the edge of the Shenandoah, Patrick's *Inn at Little Washington Cookbook* is a reasonable substitute.

PATRICK'S LOBSTER OMELETTE

For a two-egg omelette to serve one, whisk two eggs in a small bowl with a tablespoon of water, a few grains of sea salt, and a dash of white pepper. In a small sauté pan, melt a chunk of butter and warm a tablespoon of finely chopped shallot and enough coarsely chopped cooked lobster to fill a two-egg omelette. If you warm a little extra, serve it alongside the omelette. Then, in a seven-inch sauté pan (I use Teflon; Patrick, a purist, does not), melt a tablespoon of butter and, tipping the pan this way and that, spread the butter across the bottom and along the sides. You may prefer to do this by holding the butter with a fork and painting the pan with the melting butter. Patrick holds his pan over a flame. I improvise a bain-marie by placing a pan over a pot of simmering water. In either case, the pan should not be too hot. As soon as the butter foams and gives out its aroma, add the eggs and scramble them with a fork. When the curds mount up nicely, stop stirring and remove the pan from the heat. If you are using a non-Teflon pan, gently loosen the eggs from the pan with a rubber spatula. Sprinkle a vertical row of grated white cheddar through the diameter of the omelette. Top the cheese with the lobster/shallot mixture, and cover with another sprinkling of cheddar. Patrick folds the omelette neatly, like a letter, by bringing the bottom of the egg mixture to the middle of the pan and folding the top of the mixture down, to make a flat package with a seam. He then plates the elegant omelette seam side down. Since I'm not serving paying guests, I simply roll the omelette with its filling up with a fork and slide it onto a plate. The salsa is a little diced red, yellow, and green bell pepper with some diced red onion marinated for a half 'hour or so in equal parts balsamic vinegar and spicy olive oil and lightly warmed. Salt and pepper to taste. Spread the salsa along the length of the omelette, and place any extra lobster at the side.

TEN

LAST
RESORTS

When I find myself overwhelmed by human folly and the idiocy of nations, I think of exile. My first choice is Iceland, the homeland of my dear friends Ana and Olaf Olafsson and their children, Ollie, Arni, and Soley. Olaf is Iceland's leading novelist and lives in Sag Harbor. He spends his weekdays in Manhattan, where he works for a large media conglomerate. On holidays and in summer, the family goes home to Iceland, some four and a half hours east of New York, whose three hundred thousand citizens share their island with five thousand elves and five hundred thousand sheep. The latter they consume at an annual rate of fifty-five pounds per capita, more than a pound a week. Americans eat a mere pound of lamb a year. But in Iceland eating lamb is an ecological necessity. Iceland's multitudinous sheep are depleting the island's fragile ground cover of grass, moss, sedge, and berries. This forage lends the lamb its fine flavor, but also keeps the island's thin and irreplaceable topsoil from blowing out to sea. For Icelanders, eating lamb is a matter of survival. The free-range newborns left to roam each spring upon the mountain meadows are as delicately flavored, tender, and greaseless as the salt-meadow lambs of France. Smaller than either French or American lamb, Icelandic lamb lacks the heft and intensity Americans are used to, but this is a fair exchange for its delicate purity. Since Iceland derives most of its energy from the geothermal dome upon which the island sits, its atmosphere is uncorrupted by hydrocarbons. The shellfish, haddock, cod, and halibut from its clean waters are its major export. So far, the usually resourceful Icelanders have not marketed their surplus lamb as a delicacy, but now that their economy has been badly wounded by the banking crisis, perhaps they will turn to their lambs to restore their capital.

Icelanders, descendants of medieval Norsemen whose ancient language they still speak, are not as insular as one might think of an island people in the remote North Atlantic, just beneath the Arctic Circle. Culturally, they are self-sufficient, from long experience of fending for themselves on rugged ground and perilous seas, a far more difficult habitat than North American settlers faced. The first thing one notices upon arriving in Iceland is that neither space nor emotion is wasted. The architecture is unembellished. The towns are shipshape. There must be rich Icelanders and poor Icelanders, and more of the latter since the collapse of Iceland's economy, but the distinction between them and their neighborhoods is invisible, at least to strangers. The Icelandic manner is confident, welcoming, but reserved: the humor of survivors living on the world's fragile edge. This reticence may explain why Icelandic lamb is little known to the outside world.

Iceland's rates of life expectancy and literacy are higher than those of the United States. With a population two-thirds the size of the New York City borough of Staten Island, Iceland has its own international and domestic airline, a resident opera company from which it exports tenors to La Scala and other companies, a famous rock star (Björk), a world-class novelist (Olaf Olafsson), a symphony orchestra, and until Halldór Laxness died ten years ago, a Nobel laureate in literature. Reykjavik, the capital, where about a third of Icelanders live, has nine theaters, and thirty or so restaurants, not including fast-food outlets. The Hotel Holt, with its first-class restaurant, is a member of Relais & Châteaux. Reykjavik has more bookstores than I could count, and several publishing companies putting out about a thousand new titles a year. Nearly all Icelanders belong to the national church, but perhaps a third of the population believe in elves or hesitate to admit that they don't. Iceland has a coast guard to rescue fishermen in distress and protect its fishing grounds, but no army, navy, or air force. It has no enemies or spheres of influence. Until the banking crisis it was the fourth-most-productive economy per capita in the world, and the fourth-happiest.

When I visited Iceland some ten years ago with Olaf, I knew nothing about the local cuisine and expected less from such a barren country. I had heard that the shepherds entertain themselves on long winter nights by retelling the Sagas and feasting on rotten shark, but Olaf says this isn't true. Icelanders no longer eat rotten shark. Iceland grows its own vegetables, and even bananas in greenhouses heated by its geothermal springs. The sight of a sleek trawler unloading fresh cod and haddock and a flock of pint-size sheep blocking traffic gave me further hope. That night we dined on ptarmigan and reindeer at the Hotel Holt, and the following afternoon shopped for our dinner at a supermarket. Icelandic lamb racks are boned, the loins and tenderloins sold separately. We bought some of each, took them home, and browned them in butter, finishing the loins in the oven to barely medium rare. The tenderloins, about three and a half ounces each, we served from the pan with Icelandic boiled potatoes, caramelized in butter and sugar. We arranged the loins on a platter with local greens.

A few months later, in Sag Harbor at dinner with the Olafssons and friends, we began with Icelandic langoustes, which Olaf had ordered from Iceland the day before along with five pounds of lamb and some fish. We napped the langoustes with garlic-infused butter and followed them with bits of steamed cod and haddock caught in Iceland the day before, and then the lamb, sautéed quickly in butter and a little salt with a dab of rosemary-infused demi-glace, barely thickened with a trace of arrowroot. With the lamb we served some fresh peas and roasted tomatoes. Our neighbor Sheila Lukens, with her sixth sense of what goes with what, supplied three bottles of Bandol Rosé (Domaine Tempier).

To protect Iceland's delicate soil, the lamb population has been reduced by 15 percent since 1990, but the government still fails to promote its surplus overseas as a delicacy, the Kobe beef of lamb. The loins, together with the smaller tenderloins, are sold boned and fresh from September to early November, when the six-month-old lambs are butchered. Since there's no way to house the flocks over the winter, they are sold the rest of the year frozen, which does not affect their flavor or texture.

ICELANDIC LAMB

For our dinner for six, we sautéed in butter three pounds of boned loins, about three ounces each, and tenderloins, one to two ounces each, and made a light sauce of shallots, cooked in butter until softened, then dusted with arrowroot to make a light roux. We added half a bottle of Pinot Noir, which we reduced by half, and poured in seven ounces of veal and duck demi-glace (ordered from dartagnan.com), and reduced the mixture again by half, until it had just begun to thicken, then turned off the flame and steeped a branch of rosemary in the sauce. The shelled peas we cooked without water (see page 19), and we roasted six medium tomatoes from the garden until

soft in a 350-degree oven with fresh thyme, chopped garlic
softened in a little olive oil, and a sprinkling of sugar.

A few years ago, our friend Frances Cook, who was
then United States ambassador to Oman, invited us to
stay with her in Muscat, the capital of this enchanting if
reclusive sultanate at the opposite side of the world from
Iceland. Oman, on the Arabian Sea, tucked between the
United Arab Emirates, to the north, and Yemen, two
thousand miles to the south, somewhat resembles the
state of California. It has occurred to me amid our wars
and rumors of war that Iceland in summer and Oman in
winter might offer a decent refuge, assuming a few air-
lines survive the world's meander toward chaos. Here
the language is Arabic and the religion Islam, but English is taught as a second language in a thousand state
schools, and the Omani version of Islam—Ibadhism—
preaches justice, tolerance, and nonviolence. Omanis
may wear what they please. Men wear Western clothes
or traditional Arab robes and turbans. Women's tribal
dress can be elaborate: fine gold-shot cotton, or embroi-
dered caftans of a heavy material often accented with
gold coins. Under a blazing sun one day in the otherwise empty rose and golden desert, I saw an Omani
woman wearing a tribal half-mask, dressed in a gold-
trimmed caftan. With a long stick she was herding a
flock of twenty or so black goats, a magnificent sight
against the yellow sands. Tribal masks are optional but
discouraged by the government, which is aggressively
modernizing against the day, not far off, when the oil is

gone. Omanis in the eighteenth century controlled the East African coast as far south as Zanzibar, where they added cloves and sugar to the island's native pepper crop and ran a flourishing spice trade. Omanis also dominated the East African slave trade, specializing, I was told, in Ethiopian women, valued for their beauty, which may explain the Omanis' often startling good looks. This opulent past colors Oman's oil-rich present with soft infusions of old colors, textures, and tastes. Even today you can walk along the shore at Salalah, Oman's southern port, which served the China trade four centuries ago, and find undisturbed shards of centuries-old Chinese blue and white porcelain strewn on the beach, or you might wait in Salalah's modern airport beside a young Bedouin woman in a birdlike silver half-mask, the silken cuffs of an expensive blouse visible against her hennaed wrists and delicate hands resting on her smart black caftan trimmed in gold coins.

When Judy and I landed at Muscat, after an overnight flight from London, we were puzzled to find that, once we had cleared Immigration and still in our morning jet-lag fog, we were led, without explanation, by an official out to the tarmac, where Frances and a pair of helicopter pilots awaited us under a hot morning sun. As I tried to orient myself, I saw through the shimmering heat a 747 rumbling to a stop on the runway, turning 180 degrees and rumbling back the other way. Frances said, "It's the Sultan's. He doesn't like to use it, but owning a 747 is obligatory for sultans. Our sultan has two of them. The pilots are taking this one out for its morning exercise."

Still in a daze, we were now in an Omani Air Force helicopter rising into the Jebal Akhdar, the formidable Green Mountain Range that looms over Muscat. The mountains are rugged, steep, sharp-edged, inaccessible, beautiful, menacing. We came to earth on a high meadow. My ears popped as Judy, Frances, and I stepped out of the helicopter and followed the pilots toward a low-slung stone villa painted white, facing a green lawn and a screen of young fruit trees in bloom, against a Magritte-blue sky. I was told that we were at the rest house of the minister of defense in the mountain village of Saiq and were expected for lunch. The air force cook, Frances said, was formidable, envied by the other services. I was now thoroughly disoriented. What brought me around was a glorious display of local fruit—apricots, pomegranates, dates, melon, grapes—on a table under an awning on the tile patio. Lunch with the handsome air force officers was an unctuous chicken curry whose components I could only begin to parse. This was followed by a pit-roasted goat. I glimpsed our chef at the kitchen door, barely five feet in height, with the handlebar mustache of a sergeant major, a broad smile, and a white Nehru cap.

I had eaten roast goat many times in New York's barrio and in Mexico, where villagers still wrap the quartered animal in banana leaves, tie it in a basket of palm fronds, and bury it overnight in a smoldering fire pit, so that on the following day the spiced meat falls away in caramelized shreds. Our Omani chef followed the same procedures. This fire-pit cookery was probably brought to the New World by the conquistadors, whose Spanish ancestors had themselves been conquered some nine hundred years earlier by Muslim Arabs, whose desert cuisine, along with their genes, had mingled for centuries with those of the Spanish. It is this desert cookery, introduced to the New World by the gold-crazed Spanish as they stumbled toward what is now Kansas, that probably became the ancestor of today's slow-cooked, spicy barbecue, the brash New World descendant of our Omani chef's fugue of melted dates, powdered cloves, cardamom, cumin, cinnamon, and black pepper, the treasure of Oman's long Zanzibar sojourn.

New World goat in the Hispanic style can be agreeable when it is served moist and not overdone or heavily spiced, but the meltingly tender goat that we ate on the Jebel Akhdar that April afternoon, when the apricot and pomegranate blossoms trembled on our mountain meadow against an impossibly blue sky, was nothing like it. I was reminded of another April day, in 1954, in Rome, when in the Piazza Navona Barbara and I first tasted the slow-roasted unweaned lamb that the Romans eat at Easter and call *abbacchio,* whose traditional method of preparation probably descended from the Arab or perhaps Indian original. In Rome, the lamb is not dry-roasted in a fire pit but slowly braised in an oven.

This preparation, in which the slightly caramelized meat falls away from the bone, like that of a braised shoulder or shank rather than the traditionally pinkish leg of lamb, must have been practiced long before recorded history, when fuel was more valuable than time, and parsimonious cooks conserved the heat of a wood fire by smothering the embers with earth and relying upon the stone lining of the pit to release its heat slowly through the night. Today this technique can be approximated by slow braising in a heavy covered pot, either on the stovetop or in the oven, which is how the Roman cooks must have prepared our memorable *abbacchio.*

Back in New York at Eastertime after our Omani adventure, I did not dig a hole in the garden, line it with stones, and roast a goat overnight. I did, however, order from my Italian butcher a fifteen-pound lamb. Since these are not likely to be widely available, a twenty-pound spring lamb will do. The preparation is simple, but first the cook must deal with the problem of squeamishness among guests, who may recoil from young lamb as if it were the family poodle. Surely it is not an act of kindness to kill an innocent young lamb, but neither is it kind to kill the pigs that end up in our BLTs. We are omnivores, and in our various cultures—or under extreme conditions in all cultures—we will eat almost anything. In China, where snake soup is a popular restorative, the Chow dog—as in "chow mein" or "chow line"—was bred for the wok, and rats, according to the novelist Patrick O'Brian, were avidly hunted and eaten by Royal Navy midshipmen during the Napoleonic Wars, and surely by their counterparts in other navies throughout history. In my own Chinatown neighborhood, innocent frogs sit in barrels, unaware of the cleaver that awaits them; the French joyously swallow entire buntings in a single bite. Only unwavering vegetarians are entitled to deplore well-prepared infant lamb, but their complaint, though admirable, will not spare the life of a single edible creature.

If you are not handy with a cleaver and saw, ask your butcher to split the lamb in two lengthwise and divide each leg in three pieces and each shoulder in two, leaving a few ribs attached. Then divide the remainder of the rack and the saddle into four pieces. Following a recipe by Marcia Dorr in *A Taste of Oman,* I made a rub of equal amounts of powdered cinnamon, cumin, cloves, and cardamom sufficient to cover the pieces of

BRAISED YOUNG LAMB

lamb, added half as much fresh-ground black pepper as each spice, and let the lamb rest in this rub for two hours or so. The previous night, I had soaked two pounds of pitted dates in water to cover, and in the morning ran the softened dates through a food processor, adding maybe a half-cup of Omani date syrup—an optional ingredient which may not be easily available outside of Oman. In a heavy kettle, I browned the lamb in two cups of peanut oil, poured off and discarded most of the oil, removed the lamb, and threw in the puréed dates and syrup, a cup each of lemon juice and sherry vinegar, and some sea salt, and reduced the liquid by half. Then I checked the salt again, arranged the lamb in two layers, covered the pot, leaving the lid slightly ajar, and braised the lamb over a medium-low flame, turning the pieces from time to time so as not to scorch it. I checked the lamb occasionally for tenderness and to make sure that the liquid had not evaporated. If it had evaporated, I would have added a little water. After an hour or so, the meat was caramelized and falling off the bone.

PURÉED PARSNIPS I served it with three pounds of parsnips, which I cut in chunks and boiled till tender, then puréed in a food processor with a cup of half and half and a touch of powdered ginger.

My friend and neighbor Sheila Lukens contributed two bottles of a fine Mt. Eden Syrah, and so ten of us celebrated the annual rebirth of the land in Omani style, more or less.

ELEVEN

WHY
WE
EAT

Strip away the trimmings and you will find that all living things, from dainty amoeba to lumbering elephant, from wiry Barack Obama to leafy maple, share a common structure: an alimentary system supporting a reproductive apparatus. Why this of all possible arrangements should be our fate is anybody's guess. But it is plain that in the great game of survival every living thing requires nourishment in order to replicate itself and defend the tenuous grip of its species on its place in nature. Because survival demands excess, fussy feeders and reluctant breeders vanish from the gene pool, leaving stronger appetites in charge: witness the maple feasting on sunlight, then showering its multitudinous seed on the ground, or the voracious trout and its redundant spawn, or the human obsession with these twin excesses, haunting our dreams, stories, art, and music.

All other living things rely on instinct or design to

govern their hunger and lust, for unregulated desire means conflict, corruption of the habitat, and eventual extinction. The isolated forest regulates itself. The lion takes a zebra from its herd, shares it with its pride, then sleeps like its pussycat cousin sated on Purina as the herd moves on, food for another day. But when human beings encounter a pretty face or fowl, external constraints are needed. Hence our collective submission, older than recorded time, to priests, magistrates, and sacred texts to curb desire: a survival strategy embedded in ritual, law, and conscience called civilization. This uniquely human condition is foreshadowed in the expulsion of our ancestral parents from their garden of primal instinct and thrust into lives of self-denial—of either/or—a burden and an opportunity devolved upon their progeny to the present day.

In my own case, some years ago I put myself in the hands of a physician famous for curing addictions. His technique, with the help of a hypnotic drug and a rumored cattle prod, was to associate the unwanted appetite with unpleasantness, and so for several years thereafter I dined parsimoniously until the treatment failed, for eating is not an addiction, like drugs or tobacco, that can be squelched outright. Later I turned to the late Dr. Atkins and lost twenty pounds in two months of carbohydrate starvation—only to gain ten back a month later and the rest a bit more eventually.

From my Atkins adventure I contracted a few lasting aversions: pretzels, which I never liked anyway, and

bagels, with their forty grams of densely packed carbohydrates. But I see no reason to eschew the wild Baltic
salmon from Russ & Daughters or Lombardi's pizza or
Di Palo's incomparable gorgonzola dolce on a Tuscan
cracker. Perhaps my New York neighborhood with its
multitudinous temptations is at fault. But I chose to live
here. There is no escaping one's self.

I began this book in the blueberry season when I vio-
lated my vow to forgo another pie and ready myself for
a year of abstinence. Now it is apple time and my
resolve has again failed. I have baked a tarte tatin and
will not pretend to bake no more. Tarte tatin can also be
made with pears (comice are best, just as they begin to
ripen). For the traditional tarte tatin, however, you must

TARTE TATIN use apples, preferably Golden Delicious, which are not good eaten raw but hold their shape nicely in a tart. The tarte tatin is baked upside down, with the apples under the crust, which, when the finished tart is flipped, becomes the bottom. I peel, core, and quarter four Golden Delicious apples. Then, in the copper tatin pan that I bought from Fred Bridge fifty years ago, I caramelize a half-cup or so of granulated sugar in a quarter-stick of unsalted butter until the sugar becomes the color of honey. Be careful not to cook the caramel for more than a few seconds beyond this stage or the sugar will darken too much. You can move the caramel with a wooden spoon to even the color, which will be a lit-tle darker in some places than others. Then turn off the flame and wipe the wooden spoon clean (or the sugar will harden and stick to it). Carefully, for the caramel is burning hot, lay the apple wedges thick side down in a circle on the caramel, shaping one of the quarters to fill the center of the circle. Use any remaining scraps to fill gaps and sprinkle a good handful of arrowroot over the apples to hold the syrup. Now make a crust of simple pie dough by spinning in a food processor two cups of all-purpose flour with a stick of unsalted butter cut into chunks until the butter is incorporated but still a little lumpy. Then add a half-cup or a little less of ice water, a sprinkle at a time, processing after each addition, until the dough begins to form. As soon as it forms, remove it from the processor onto a marble slab or plastic sheet, and knead the dough into an oblong. You might enclose the dough in plastic wrap at this point and let it rest in the refrigerator for a half hour or so to relax the gluten, or you can skip this step, as I usually do. Then roll out the dough in a circle about an eighth of an inch thick, place the tarte pan with its apples (or pears) adjacent to the dough, roll the dough onto the rolling pin, and place it over the apples, discarding the trimmings or saving them for another purpose. With a fork I tuck the edge of the dough down into the pan. Then I slip the pie onto the middle shelf of an oven just under 360 degrees, at which temperature the fruit will not stick to the pan when you turn it right side up. But if you forget and some of the slices stick, just shove them with a wooden spoon from the pan into the gaps where they belong and smooth everything out. When the crust begins to darken, after about forty minutes, slip the pie out of the oven and let it cool for ten minutes or so. Then carefully place the plate on which you plan to serve the tarte over the pastry and flip the pie over. If the syrup is still runny, spoon it back over the pie and with a damp paper towel wipe up any excess syrup from the serving plate. A dedicated tarte tatin pan is not essential. A well-seasoned iron skillet or even an eight-inch sauté pan will do just as well. Serve the tarte warm with vanilla ice cream.

And so life goes on.

INDEX

A NOTE ABOUT THE AUTHOR

Jason Epstein has led one of the most creative careers in book publishing of the past half century. In 1952, while a young editor at Doubleday, he created Anchor Books, which launched the so-called paperback revolution and established the trade-paperback format. In the following decade, he became cofounder of *The New York Review of Books*. In the 1980s, he created the Library of America, the prestigious publisher of American classics, and The Reader's Catalog, the precursor of online bookselling. For many years, Jason Epstein was editorial director of Random House. He was the first recipient of the National Book Award for Distinguished Service to American Letters, and he has been given the Curtis Benjamin Award of the Association of American Publishers for "inventing new kinds of publishing and editing" as well as the Lifetime Achievement Award of the National Book Critic's Circle and the Philolexian Award for Distinguished Literary Achievement. He has edited many well-known novelists, including Norman Mailer, Vladimir Nabokov, E. L. Doctorow, Peter Matthiessen, Philip Roth, and Gore Vidal, as well as many important writers of nonfiction.